COMPUTER ATTACK AND CYBERTERRORISM

CLAY WILSON

Nova Science Publishers, Inc.
New York

LIBRARY OF CONGRESS CATALOGING-IN-PUBLICATION DATA

1007522587

ISBN 978-1-60692-337-5

Available upon rerquest

Published by Nova Science Publishers, Inc. New York

CONTENTS

PREFACE

Many international terrorist groups now actively use computers and the Internet to communicate, and several may develop or acquire the necessary technical skills to direct a coordinated attack against computers in the United States. A cyberattack intended to harm the U.S. economy would likely target computers that operate the civilian critical infrastructure and government agencies. However, there is disagreement among some observers about whether a coordinated cyberattack against the U.S. critical infrastructure could be extremely harmful, or even whether computers operating the civilian critical infrastructure actually offer an effective target for furthering terrorists' goals.

While there is no published evidence that terrorist organizations are currently planning a coordinated attack against computers, computer system vulnerabilities persist worldwide, and initiators of the random cyberattacks that plague computers on the Internet remain largely unknown. Reports from security organizations show that random attacks are now increasingly implemented through use of automated tools, called "bots", that direct large numbers of compromised computers to launch attacks through the Internet as swarms. The growing trend toward the use of more automated attack tools has also overwhelmed some of the current methodologies used for tracking Internet cyberattacks.

This report provides background information for three types of attacks against computers (cyberattack, physical attack, and electromagnetic attack), and discusses related vulnerabilities for each type of attack. The report also describes the possible effects of a coordinated cyberattack, or computer network attack (CNA), against U.S. infrastructure computers, along with possible technical capabilities of international terrorists.

Issues for Congress may include how could trends in cyberattacks be measured more effectively; what is appropriate guidance for DOD use of cyberweapons; should cybersecurity be combined with, or remain separate from, the physical security organization within DHS; how can commercial vendors be encouraged to improve the security of their products; and what are options to encourage U.S. citizens to follow better cybersecurity practices?

Appendices to this report describe computer viruses, spyware, and "bot networks", and how malicious programs are used to enable cybercrime and cyberespionage. Also, similarities are drawn between planning tactics currently used by computer hackers and those used by terrorists groups for conventional attacks.

Chapter 1

INTRODUCTION

Many Pentagon officials reportedly believe that future adversaries may resort to strategies intended to offset U.S. military technological superiority.[1] Because the U.S. military is supported in significant ways by civilian high technology products and services (including communications systems, electronics, and computer software), future conflicts may involve a blurring of the distinction between civilian and military targets.[2] Therefore, civilian systems, including computers that operate the U.S. critical infrastructure, may increasingly be seen as viable targets that are vulnerable to attack by adversaries, including terrorist groups.

Some feel that past discussions about a coordinated attack against civilian computers may have over-inflated the perceived risk to the U.S. critical infrastructure, and several experts have stated that cyberterrorism does not pose the same type of threat as Nuclear, Biological, or Chemical (NBC) threats.[3] Many experts also believe that it would be difficult to use attacks against computers to inflict death on a large scale, and have stated that conventional physical threats present a much more serious concern for U.S. national security.[4] However, other observers point out that terrorist groups now use the Internet to communicate via websites, chat rooms, and email, to raise funds, and to covertly gather intelligence on future targets. From these activities, it is evident that the knowledge that terrorist groups' have of computer technology is increasing, and along with that, a better knowledge of related vulnerabilities. Should any terrorist groups initiate a coordinated attack against computer systems in the United States, most security experts agree that the likely scenario would be to try to disable U.S. computers or communications systems so as to amplify the effects of, or supplement, a conventional terrorist bombing or other major NBC attack.

Congress may wish to explore the possible effects on the U.S. economy and on the U.S. military that might result from a coordinated attack against civilian computers and communications systems. Congress may also wish to explore options for protecting civilian computer systems against a coordinated attack and the possible international consequences that might result from any U.S. military response to such an attack.

The Background section of this report describes three methods for attacking computers; however, the report focuses on the method most commonly known as cyberattack or computer network attack (CNA), which involves disruption caused by malicious computer code. It also describes the current disagreement over the possible effects of a coordinated cyberattack on the U.S. critical infrastructure, and why the random cyberattacks that plague the Internet continue to be successful. There is also a brief discussion about the possible capabilities of terrorist groups and terrorist-sponsoring nations to initiate a coordinated cyberattack.

Three appendices give a description of the tactics possibly used in planning and executing a computer network attack.

Chapter 2

BACKGROUND

The focus of this report is possible cyberterrorism using computer network attack, or cyberattack. However, when IT facilities and computer equipment are deliberately targeted by a terrorist group, it is possible that a physical attack, or an electronic attack (EA), may also fit within one or more of the expert definitions shown below for "cyberterrorism."

THREE METHODS FOR COMPUTER ATTACK

A computer attack may be defined as actions directed against computer systems to disrupt equipment operations, change processing control, or corrupt stored data. Different attack methods target different vulnerabilities and involve different types of weapons, and several may be within the current capabilities of some terrorist groups.[5] Three different methods of attack are identified in this report, based on the effects of the weapons used. However, as technology evolves, distinctions between these methods may begin to blur.

- A physical attack involves conventional weapons directed against a computer facility or its transmission lines;
- An electronic attack (EA) involves the use the power of electromagnetic energy as a weapon, more commonly as an electromagnetic pulse (EMP) to overload computer circuitry, but also in a less violent form, to insert a stream of malicious digital code directly into an enemy microwave radio transmission; and

- A computer network attack (CNA), usually involves malicious code used as a weapon to infect enemy computers to exploit a weakness in software, in the system configuration, or in the computer security practices of an organization or computer user. Other forms of CNA are enabled when an attacker uses stolen information to enter restricted computer systems.

DOD officials have stated that while CNA and EA threats are "less likely" than physical attacks, they could actually prove more damaging because they involve disruptive technologies that might generate unpredictable consequences or give an adversary unexpected advantages.[6]

Characteristics of Physical Attack.

A physical attack disrupts the reliability of computer equipment and availability of data. Physical attack is implemented either through use of conventional weapons, creating heat, blast, and fragmentation, or through direct manipulation of wiring or equipment, usually after gaining unauthorized physical access.

In 1991, during Operation Desert Storm, the U.S. military reportedly disrupted Iraqi communications and computer centers by sending cruise missiles to scatter carbon filaments that short circuited power supply lines. Also, the Al Qaeda attacks directed against the World Trade Center and the Pentagon on September 11, 2001, destroyed many important computer databases and disrupted civilian and military financial and communications systems that were linked globally.[7] The temporary loss of communications links and important data added to the effects of the physical attack by closing financial markets for up to a week.[8]

Characteristics of Electronic Attack (EA)

Electronic attack, most commonly referred to as an Electromagnetic Pulse (EMP), disrupts the reliability of electronic equipment through generating instantaneous high energy that overloads circuit boards, transistors, and other electronics.[9] EMP effects can penetrate computer facility walls where they can erase electronic memory, upset software, or permanently disable all electronic components.[10] Some assert that little has been done by the private sector to protect against the threat from electromagnetic pulse, and that commercial electronic systems in the United States could be severely damaged by limited range, small-scale, or portable electromagnetic pulse devices.[11] Some military experts have stated that the United States is perhaps the nation most vulnerable to electromagnetic pulse attack.[12]

A Commission to Assess the Threat from High Altitude Electromagnetic Pulse was established by Congress in FY2001 after several experts expressed concern that the U.S. critical infrastructure and military were vulnerable to high altitude EMP attack.[13] At a July 22, 2004, hearing before the House Armed Services Committee, panel members from the Commission reportedly stated that as more U.S. military weapons and control systems become increasingly complex, they may also be more vulnerable to the effects of EMP. The consensus of the Commission is that a large-scale high altitude EMP attack could possibly hold our society seriously at risk and might result in defeat of our military forces.[14]

However, the Department of Homeland Security (DHS) has stated that testing of the current generation of civilian core telecommunications switches now in use has shown that they are only minimally affected by EMP. DHS has also stated that most of the core communications assets for the United States are housed in large, very well constructed facilities which provide a measure of shielding against the effects of EMP.[15]

Observers believe that mounting a coordinated attack against U.S. computer systems, using either larger-scale, smaller-scale, or even portable EMP weapons requires technical skills that are beyond the capabilities of most terrorist organizations. However, nations such as Russia, and possibly terrorist-sponsoring nations such as North Korea, now have the technical capability to construct and deploy a smaller chemically-driven, or battery-driven EMP device that could disrupt computers at a limited range.[16]

For more on electromagnetic weapons, see CRS Report RL32544, *High Altitude Electromagnetic Pulse (HEMP) and High Power Microwave (HPM) Devices: Threat Assessments.*

Characteristics of Cyberattack (CNA)

A computer network attack (CNA), or "cyberattack," disrupts the integrity or authenticity of data, usually through malicious code that alters program logic that controls data, leading to errors in output (for more detail, see Appendices A, B, and C). Computer hackers opportunistically scan the Internet looking for computer systems that are mis-configured or lacking necessary security software.

Once infected with malicious code, a computer can be remotely controlled by a hacker who may, via the Internet, send commands to spy on the contents of that computer or attack and disrupt other computers.

Cyberattacks usually require that the targeted computer have some pre-existing system flaw, such as a software error, a lack of antivirus protection, or a faulty system configuration, for the malicious code to exploit. However, as technology evolves, this distinguishing requirement of CNA may begin to fade. For example, some forms of EA can now cause effects nearly identical to some forms of CNA. For example, at controlled power levels, the transmissions between targeted microwave radio towers can be hijacked and specially designed viruses, or altered code, can be inserted directly into the adversary's digital network.[17]

IDENTIFYING CYBERTERRORISM

No single definition of the term "terrorism" has yet gained universal acceptance. Likewise, no single definition for the term "cyberterrorism" has been universally accepted. Labeling a computer attack as "cyberterrorism" is problematic because of the difficulty determining the identity, intent, or the political motivations of an attacker with certainty.

Under 22 USC, section 2656, "terrorism" is defined as premeditated, politically motivated violence perpetrated against noncombatant targets by sub national groups or clandestine agents, usually intended to influence an audience.[18]

Expert Opinions Differ

Some definitions for cyberterrorism focus on the intent of the attackers. For example, the Federal Emergency Management Agency (FEMA) defines cyberterrorism as: "Unlawful attacks and threats of attack against computers, networks, and the information stored therein when done to intimidate or coerce a government or its people in furtherance of political or social objectives."[19] Security expert Dorothy Denning defines cyberterrorism as the "politically motivated hacking operations intended to cause grave harm such as loss of life or severe economic damage."[20] Others assert that any deliberate use of information technology by terrorist groups and their agents to cause harm constitutes cyberterrorism.[21]

Some security experts define cyberterrorism based on the effects of an attack. Included are activities where computers are targeted and the resulting effects are destructive or disruptive enough to generate fear potentially comparable to that from a traditional act of terrorism, even if initiated by criminals with no political motive. Under this "effects" view, even computer attacks that are limited in scope, but lead to death, injury, extended power outages, airplane crashes, water contamination, or major loss of confidence for portions of the economy, may also be labeled cyberterrorism.[22] Some observers state that cyberterrorism can take the form of a physical attack that destroys computerized nodes for critical infrastructures, such as the Internet, telecommunications, or the electric power grid, without ever touching a keywboard.[23] DHS officials have also asserted that cybersecurity cuts across all aspects of critical infrastructure protection and that cyberoperations cannot be separated from the physical aspects of businesses because they operate interdependently.[24]

Thus, where computers or IT facilities and equipment are deliberately targeted by terrorist groups, methods involving physical attack and EA may each fit within the above definitions for "cyberterrorism."

Cyberterrorism Defined

By combining the above concepts of intent and effects, "cyberterrorism" may be defined as the use of computers as weapons, or as targets, by politically motivated international, or sub-national groups, or clandestine agents who threaten or cause violence and fear in order to influence an audience, or cause a government to change its policies. This definition, which combines several opinions about cyberterrorism, can encompass all three methods: physical, EA, and CNA, for attacks against computers.

Difficulty Identifying Attackers

Instructions for exploiting computer vulnerabilities are easily obtainable by anyone via the Internet. However, to date, there is no published evidence linking a sustained or widespread attack using CNA with international terrorist groups.[25] It remains difficult to determine the identity of the initiators of most cyberattacks, while at the same time security organizations continue to report that computer virus attacks are becoming more frequent, causing more economic losses, and affecting larger areas of the globe. For example, the Computer Emergency Response Team Coordination Center (CERT/CC) shows that 137,529 computer security incidents were reported to their office in 2003, up from 82,094 in 2002.[26] The challenge of identifying the source of attacks is complicated by the unwillingness of commercial enterprises to report attacks, owing to potential liability concerns. CERT/CC estimates that as much as 80% of all actual computer security incidents still remain unreported.[27]

POSSIBLE EFFECTS OF CYBERTERRORISM

As yet, no coordinated or widespread cyberattack has had a crippling effect on the U.S. infrastructure. However, while the number of random Internet cyberattacks has been increasing, the data collected to measure the trends for cyberattacks cannot be used to accurately determine if a terrorist group, or terrorist-sponsoring state, has initiated any of them.

A recent private study found that during the latter half of 2002, the highest rates for global cyberattack activity were directed against critical infrastructure industry companies.[28] A new report on industrial cybersecurity problems, produced by the British Columbia Institute of Technology, and the PA Consulting Group, using data from as far back as 1981, reportedly has found a 10-fold increase in the number of successful cyberattacks on infrastructure Supervisory Control And Data Acquisition systems since 2000.[29] DOD officials have also observed that the number of attempted intrusions into military networks has gradually increased, from 40,076 incidents in 2001, to 43,086 in 2002, 54,488 in 2003, and 24,745 as of June 2004.[30] The consequences of these attacks on military operations are not clear, however.

Disagreement about Effects on the Critical Infrastructure

While security experts agree that a coordinated cyberattack could be used to amplify the effects of a conventional physical terrorist attack, such as an NBC attack, many of these same experts disagree about the damaging effects that might result from an attack directed against computers that operate the U.S. critical infrastructure. Some observers have stated that because of U.S. dependency on computer technology, such attacks may have the potential to create economic damage on a large scale, while other observers have stated that U.S. infrastructure systems are resilient and would possibly recover easily, thus avoiding any severe or catastrophic effects.

Some of China's military journals speculate that cyberattacks could disable American financial markets. China, however, is as dependent on these markets as the United States, and could suffer even more from their disruption. As to other critical infrastructures, the amount of potential damage that could be inflicted may be relatively trivial compared to the costs of discovery, if engaged in by a nation state. These constraints, however, do not apply to non-state actors like Al Qaeda, making cyberattacks a potentially useful tool for it and others who reject the global market economy. [31]

In July 2002, the U.S. Naval War College hosted a war game called "Digital Pearl Harbor" to develop a scenario for a coordinated cyberterrorism event, where mock attacks by computer security experts against critical infrastructure systems simulated state-sponsored cyberwarfare. The simulated cyberattacks determined that the most vulnerable infrastructure computer systems were the Internet itself, and the computer systems that are part of the financial infrastructure.[32] It was also determined that attempts to cripple the U.S. telecommunications infrastructure would be unsuccessful because system redundancy would prevent damage from becoming too widespread. The conclusion of the exercise was that a "Digital Pearl Harbor" in the United States was only a slight possibility.[33]

However, in 2002, a major vulnerability was discovered in switching equipment software that threatened the infrastructure for major portions of the Internet. A flaw in the Simple Network Management Protocol (SNMP) would have enabled attackers to take over Internet routers and cripple network telecommunications equipment globally. Network and equipment vendors worldwide raced quickly to fix their products before the problem could be exploited by hackers, with possible worldwide consequences. U.S. government officials also reportedly made efforts to keep information about this major vulnerability quiet until after the needed repairs were implemented on vulnerable Internet systems.[34] According to an assessment reportedly written by the FBI, the security flaw could have been exploited to cause many serious problems, such as bringing down widespread telephone networks and also halting control information exchanged between ground and aircraft flight control systems.[35]

Unpredictable Interactions Between Infrastructures

An important area that is not fully understood concerns the unpredictable interactions between computer systems that operate the different U.S. infrastructures. The concern is that numerous interdependencies (where downstream systems may rely on receiving good data through stable links with upstream computers in a different infrastructure) could possibly build to a cascade of damaging effects that are unpredictable in how they might affect national security.[36] For example, in 2003 while the newly released "Blaster" worm was causing disruption of Internet computers over several days in August, it may also have added to the severity of the Eastern United States power blackout that occurred on August 14, by degrading the performance of several communications lines that linked the data centers used by utility companies to send warnings to other managers downstream on the power grid.[37]

SCADA Systems May Be Vulnerable

Supervisory Control And Data Acquisition (SCADA) systems are computer systems relied upon by most critical infrastructure organizations (such as companies that manage the power grid) to automatically monitor and adjust switching, manufacturing, and other process control activities, based on digitized feedback data gathered by sensors. These control systems are frequently unmanned, operate in remote locations, and are accessed periodically by engineers or technical staff via telecommunications links.

Some experts believe that these systems may be especially vulnerable, and that their importance for controlling the critical infrastructure may make them an attractive target for cyberterrorists. SCADA systems, once connected only to isolated networks using only proprietary computer software, now operate using more vulnerable Commercial-Off-The-Shelf (COTS) software, and are increasingly being linked directly into corporate office networks via the Internet.[38] Some observers believe that many, if not most, SCADA systems are inadequately protected against a cyberattack, and remain persistently vulnerable because many organizations that operate them have not paid proper attention to their unique computer security needs.[39]

The following example may serve to illustrate the vulnerability of control systems and highlight possible cybersecurity issues that could arise for infrastructure nodes when SCADA controls are interconnected with office networks. In August 2003, the "Slammer"Internet computer worm was able to corrupt for five hours the computer control systems at the Davis-Besse nuclear power plant located in Ohio (fortunately, the power plant was closed and off-line when the cyberattack occurred). The computer worm was able to successfully penetrate systems in the Davis-Besse power plant control room largely because the business network for its corporate offices was found to have multiple connections to the Internet that bypassed the control room firewall.[40]

However, other observers suggest that SCADA systems and the critical infrastructure are more robust and resilient than early theorists of cyberterror have stated, and that the infrastructure would likely recover rapidly from a cyberterrorism attack. They cite, for example, that water system failures, power outages, air traffic disruptions, and other scenarios resembling possible cyberterrorism often occur as routine events, and rarely affect national security, even marginally. System failures due to storms routinely occur at the regional level, where service may often be denied to customers for hours or days. Technical experts who understand the systems would work to restore functions as quickly as possible. Cyberterrorists would need to attack multiple targets simultaneously for long periods of time to gradually create terror, achieve strategic goals, or to have any noticeable effects on national security.[41]

For more information about SCADA systems, see CRS Report RL31534, Critical Infrastructure: Control Systems and the Terrorist Threat.

DOD Relies on Civilian Technology

During Operation Iraqi Freedom, commercial satellites were used to supplement other military communications channels, which at times lacked sufficient capacity.[42] A cyberattack directed against civilian communications systems could possibly disrupt communications to some combat units, or could possibly lead to delayed shipment of military supplies, or a slowdown in the scheduling and deployment of troops before a crisis.

Several simulations have been conducted to determine what effects an attempted cyberattack on the critical infrastructure might have on U.S. defense systems. In 1997, DOD conducted a mock cyberattack to test the ability of DOD systems to respond to protect the national information infrastructure. That exercise, called operation "Eligible Receiver 1997," revealed dangerous vulnerabilities in U.S. military information systems.[43] In October 2002, a subsequent mock cyberattack against DOD systems, titled "Eligible Receiver 2003," indicated a need for greater coordination between military and non-military organizations to deploy a rapid military computer counter-attack.[44]

DOD also uses Commercial-Off-The-Shelf (COTS) hardware and software products both in core information technology administrative functions, and also in the combat systems of all services, as for example, in the integrated warfare systems for nuclear aircraft carriers.[45] DOD favors the use of COTS products in order to take advantage of technological innovation, product flexibility and standardization and resulting cost-effectiveness. Nevertheless, DOD officials and others have stated that COTS products are lacking in security, and that strengthening the security of those products to meet military requirements may be too difficult and costly for most COTS vendors. To improve security, DOD Information Assurance practices require deploying several layers of additional protective measures around COTS military systems to make them more difficult for enemy cyberattackers to penetrate.[46]

However, on two separate occasions in 2004, viruses reportedly infiltrated two top-secret computer systems at the Army Space and Missile Defense Command. It is not clear how the viruses penetrated the military systems, or what the effects were. Also, contrary to security policy requirements, the computers reportedly lacked basic anti virus software protection.[47] Security experts have noted that for both military and civilian systems, no matter how much protection is given to computers, hackers are always creating new ways to defeat those protective measures, and whenever systems are connected on a network, it is possible to exploit even a relatively secure system by jumping from a non-secure system.[48]

WHY CYBERATTACKS ARE SUCCESSFUL

Networked computers with exposed vulnerabilities may be disrupted or taken over by a hacker, or by automated malicious code. Should a terrorist group attempt to launch a coordinated cyberattack against computers that manage the U.S. critical infrastructure, they may find it useful to copy some of the tactics now commonly used by today's computer hacker groups to locate Internet-connected computers with vulnerabilities, and then systematically exploit those vulnerabilities (see Appendices A, B, and C).

Hackers Search for Computer System Vulnerabilities

Computer hackers opportunistically scan the Internet to find and infect computer systems that are mis-configured, or lack current software security patches. Compromised computers can become part of a "bot network" or "bot herd" (a "bot" is a remotely-controlled, or semi-autonomous computer program that can infect computers), sometimes comprised of hundred or thousands of compromised computers that can all controlled remotely by a single hacker. This "bot herd" hacker may instruct the computers through an encrypted communications channel to spy on the owner of each infected computer, and quietly transmit copies of any sensitive data that is found, or he may direct the "herd" to collectively attack as a swarm against other targeted computers.

Even computers with current software security patches installed may still be vulnerable to a type of CNA known as a "Zero-Day exploit". This may occur if a computer hacker discovers a new software vulnerability and launches a malicious attack program to infect the computer before a security patch can be created by the software vendor and distributed to protect users.

In results of a 2004 survey of security and law enforcement executives, conducted in part by the Secret Service, CSO (Chief Security Officer) magazine, and the Computer Emergency Response Team Coordination Center (CERT/CC), a major reporting center for statistics on Internet security problems, hackers are cited as the greatest cybersecurity threat. The survey also shows that while 43% of respondents reported an increase in cybercrimes over the previous year, at least 30% of those did not know whether insiders or outsiders were the cause. Of those respondents who did know, 71% of attacks reportedly came from outsiders while 29% came from insiders.[49]

Automated Cyberattacks Spread Quickly

The "Slammer" computer worm attacked Microsoft's database software and spread through the Internet over the space of one weekend in January 2003. According to a preliminary study coordinated by the Cooperative Association for Internet Data Analysis (CAIDA), on January 25, 2003, the SQL Slammer worm (also known as "Sapphire") automatically spread to infect more than 90 percent of vulnerable computers worldwide within 10 minutes of its release on the Internet, making it the fastest computer worm in history. As the study reports, exploiting a known vulnerability for which a patch has been available since July 2002, Slammer doubled in size every 8.5 seconds and achieved its full scanning rate (55 million scans per second) after about 3 minutes. It caused considerable harm through network outages and such unforeseen consequences as canceled airline flights and automated teller machine (ATM) failures.[50]

Whenever a cyberattack against computers or networks is reported to CERT/CC, it is recorded as a statistic for security incidents. However, as of 2004, CERT/CC has abandoned this practice for keeping a record of cyberattacks. This is because the widespread use of automated cyberattack tools has escalated the number of network attacks to such a high level, that their organization has stated that a count of security incidents has become meaningless as a metric for assessing the scope and effects of attacks against Internet-connected systems.[51]

Persistence of Computer System Vulnerabilities

Vulnerabilities in software and computer system configurations provide the entry points for a cyberattack. Vulnerabilities persist largely as a result of poor security practices and procedures, inadequate training in computer security, or poor quality in software products.[52] Inadequate resources devoted to staffing the security function may also contribute to poor security practices. Home computer users often have little or no training in best practices for effectively securing home networks and equipment.

Errors in New Software Products

Vendors for Commercial-Off-The-Shelf software (COTS) are often criticized for releasing new products with errors that create the computer system vulnerabilities.[53] Approximately 80 percent of successful intrusions into federal computer systems reportedly can be attributed to software errors, or poor software product quality.[54] Richard Clarke, former White House cyberspace advisor until 2003, has reportedly said that many commercial software products have poorly written, or poorly configured security features.[55] Richard D. Pethia, Director, CERT/CC, Software Engineering Institute, Carnegie Mellon University, in testimony before the House Select Committee on Homeland Security, Subcommittee on Cybersecurity, Science, and Research and Development, stated, "There is little evidence of improvement in the security features of most products; developers are not devoting sufficient effort to apply lessons learned about the sources of vulnerabilities....We continue to see the same types of vulnerabilities in newer versions of products that we saw in earlier versions. Technology evolves so rapidly that vendors concentrate on time to market, often minimizing that time by placing a low priority on security features. Until their customers demand products that are more secure, the situation is unlikely to change.[56]"

In response to complaints, the software industry reportedly has made new efforts to design software with more secure code and with architectures that are more secure. For example, Microsoft has created a special Security Response Center and now works with DOD and with industry and government leaders to improve security features in its new products. However, many software industry representatives reportedly agree that no matter what investment is made to improve software security, there will continue to be vulnerabilities found in software because it is becoming increasingly more complex.[57]

Inadequate Resources

Although software vendors periodically release fixes or upgrades to solve newly discovered security problems, an important software security patch might not get scheduled for installation on an organization's computers until several weeks or months after the patch is available.[58] The job may be too time-consuming, too complex, or too low a priority for the system administration staff. With increased software complexity comes the introduction of more vulnerabilities, so system maintenance is never-ending. Sometimes the security patch itself may disrupt the computer when installed, forcing the system administrator to take additional time to adjust the computer to accept the new patch. To avoid such disruption, a security patch may first require testing on a separate isolated network before it is distributed for installation on all other computers.

Because of such delays, the computer security patches actually installed in many organizations may lag considerably behind the current cyberthreat situation. Whenever delays are allowed to persist in private organizations, in government agencies, or among PC users at home, computer vulnerabilities that are widely reported may remain unprotected, leaving networks open to possible attack for long periods of time.

One way to improve this would be to encourage the software industry to create products that do not require system administrators to devote so much time to installing fixes. Many security experts also emphasize that if systems administrators received the necessary training for keeping their computer configurations secure, then computer security would greatly improve for the U.S. critical infrastructure.[59]

Offshore Outsourcing

Many major software companies now outsource code development to subcontractors who design and build large portions of COTS products outside the United States.[60] Offshore outsourcing may give a programmer in a foreign country the chance to secretly insert a Trojan Horse or other malicious code into a new commercial software product. GAO reportedly has begun a review of DOD reliance on foreign software development to determine the adequacy of measures intended to reduce these related security risks in commercial software products purchased for military systems.

Software industry representatives have responded by saying that offshore outsourcing should not be cited as the only possible source for malicious code. Most core software components are designed and developed within the United States, and despite the emerging controversy about security and offshore outsourcing, many software developers working and residing here also have foreign backgrounds. Therefore, to improve national security it may be more effective to focus not on the location where code is developed, but rather to focus on making certain that software vendors always have rigorous quality assurance techniques in place no matter where the code is produced. However, higher standards for quality assurance will also involve more costs and additional time for testing.[61]

For more information about offshore outsourcing and national security, see CRS Report RL32411, *Network Centric Warfare: Background and Oversight Issues for Congress*, and CRS Report RL32179, *Manufacturing Output, Productivity and Employment: Implications for U.S. Policy.*

TERRORIST CAPABILITIES FOR CYBERATTACK

Extensive planning and pre-operational surveillance by hackers are important characteristics that precede a cyberattack directed at an organization.[62] Some experts estimate that advanced or structured cyberattacks against multiple systems and networks, including target surveillance and testing of sophisticated new hacker tools, might require from two to four years of preparation, while a complex coordinated cyberattack, causing mass disruption against integrated, heterogeneous systems may require 6 to 10 years of preparation.[63] This characteristic, where hackers devote much time to detailed and extensive planning before launching a cyberattack, has also been described as a "hallmark" of previous physical terrorist attacks and bombings launched by Al Qaeda (see Appendices A and C).

Attractiveness of Cyberterrorism

It is difficult to determine the level of interest, or the capabilities of international terrorist groups to launch an effective cyberattack. A 1999 report by The Center for the Study of Terrorism and Irregular Warfare at the Naval Postgraduate School concluded that it is likely that any severe cyberattacks experienced in the near future by industrialized nations will be used by terrorist groups simply to supplement the more traditional physical terrorist attacks.[64]

Some observers have stated that Al Qaeda does not see cyberterrorism as important for achieving its goals, preferring attacks which inflict human casualties.[65] Other observers believe that the groups most likely to consider and employ cyberattack and cyberterrorism are the terrorist groups operating in post-industrial societies (such as Europe and the United States), rather than international terrorist groups that operate in developing regions where there is limited access to high technology.

However, other sources report that Al Qaeda has taken steps to improve organizational secrecy through more active and clever use of technology, and evidence suggests that Al Qaeda terrorists used the Internet extensively to plan their operations for September 11, 2001.[66] Al Qaeda cells reportedly used new Internet-based telephone services to communicate with other terrorist cells overseas. Khalid Shaikh Mohammed, one of the masterminds of the plot against the World Trade Center, reportedly used special Internet chat software to communicate with at least two airline hijackers. Ramzi Yousef, who was sentenced to life imprisonment for the previous bombing of the World Trade Center, had trained as an electrical engineer, and had planned to use sophisticated electronics to detonate bombs on 12 U.S. airliners departing from Asia for the United States. He also used sophisticated encryption to protect his data and to prevent law enforcement from reading his plans should he be captured.[67]

Lower Risk

Tighter physical security measures now widely in place throughout the United States may encourage terrorist groups in the future to explore cyberattack as way to lower the risk of detection for their operations.[68] Also, linkages between networked computers could expand the effects of a cyberattack. Therefore, a cyberattack directed against only a few vulnerable computers could multiply its effects by corrupting important information that is transmitted to other downstream businesses.

Less Dramatic

However, other security observers believe that terrorist organizations might be reluctant to launch a cyberattack because it would result in less immediate drama and have a lower psychological impact than a more conventional act of destruction, such as a bombing. These observers believe that unless a cyberattack can be made to result in actual physical damage or bloodshed, it will never be considered as serious as a nuclear, biological, or chemical terrorist attack.[69]

Links with Terrorist-Sponsoring Nations

The U.S. Department of State, as of October 2004, lists seven designated state sponsors of terrorism: Cuba, Iran, Iraq, Libya, North Korea, Syria, and Sudan.[70] These countries are identified as sponsors for funding, providing weapons, and supplying other resources used for operations by terrorist groups.

However, a study of trends in Internet attacks determined that countries that are state sponsors of terrorism generated less than one percent of all reported cyberattacks directed against selected businesses in 2002.[71] News sources have reported that, other than a few website defacements, there was no evidence that a computer attack was launched by Iraq or by terrorist organizations against United States military forces during Gulf War II.[72] The security research organization, C4I.org, reported that prior to the March 2003 deployment of U.S. troops, traffic increased from Web surfers in Iraq using search terms such as, "Computer warfare," "NASA computer network," and "airborne computer." Experts interpreted the increased Web traffic as an indication that Iraq's government was increasingly relying on the Internet for intelligence gathering.[73]

Elements in Iran are believed by some observers to have links with Al Qaeda as well as other terrorist groups, and North Korea has continued to sell weapons and high-technology items to other countries designated as state sponsors of terrorism. Other news sources have reported that North Korea may be building up their own capabilities for cyberoperations. Security experts reportedly believe that North Korea may have developed a considerable capability for cyberwarfare partly in response to South Korea's admitted build up of computer training centers and its expanding defense budget to prepare for information warfare.[74] Computer programmers from the Pyongyang Informatics Center in North Korea have done contract work to develop software for local governments and businesses in Japan and South Korea. And, recent statements made by South Korea's Defense Security Command claim that North Korea may currently be training more than 100 new computer hackers per year, for national defense.[75] However, Pentagon and State Department officials reportedly are unable to confirm the claims made by South Korea, and defense experts reportedly believe that North Korea is incapable of seriously disrupting U.S. military computer systems. Also, Department of State officials have reportedly said that North Korea is not known to have sponsored any terrorist acts since 1987.

Links Between Terrorists and Hackers

Links between computer hackers and terrorists, or terrorist-sponsoring nations may be difficult to confirm. Membership in the most highly-skilled computer hacker groups is sometimes very exclusive, limited to individuals who develop, demonstrate, and share only with each other their most closely-guarded set of sophisticated hacker tools. These exclusive hacker groups do not seek attention because maintaining secrecy allows them to operate more effectively.

Some hacker groups may also have political interests that are supra-national, or based on religion or other socio-political ideologies, while other hacker groups may be motivated by profit, or linked to organized crime, and may be willing to sell their computer services, regardless of the political interests involved. For example, it has been reported that the Indian separatist group, Harkat-ul-Ansar (an Islamic fundamentalist group in Pakistan that operates primarily in Kashmir, and is also now labeled a Foreign Terrorist Organization in 1997 for its links with bin Laden), attempted to purchase cyberattack software from hackers in late 1998. In March 2000, it was reported that the Aum Shinrikyo cult, a designated Foreign Terrorist Organization, had contracted to write software for 80 Japanese companies, and 10 government agencies, including Japan's Metropolitan Police Department; however, no cyberattacks that related to these contracts were reported.[76]

However, information about computer vulnerabilities is now for sale online in a hackers' "black market". For example, list of 5,000 addresses of computers that have already been infected with spyware and which are waiting to be remotely controlled as part of an automated "bot network" (see Appendix A) reportedly can be obtained for about $150 to $500. Prices for information about computer vulnerabilities for which no software patch yet exists reportedly range from $1,000 to $5,000. Purchasers of this information are often companies that deal in spam, organized crime groups, and various foreign governments.[77]

FEDERAL EFFORTS TO PROTECT COMPUTERS

The federal government has taken steps to improve its own computer security and to encourage the private sector to also adopt stronger computer security policies and practices to reduce infrastructure vulnerabilities. In 2002, the Federal Information Security Management Act (FISMA) was enacted, giving the Office of Management and Budget (OMB) responsibility for coordinating information security standards and guidelines developed by federal agencies.[78] In 2003, the National Strategy to Secure Cyberspace was published by the Administration to encourage the private sector to improve computer security for the U.S. critical infrastructure through having federal agencies set an example for best security practices.[79]

The National Cyber Security Division (NCSD), within the Information Analysis and Infrastructure Protection Directorate of the Department of Homeland Security (DHS) oversees a Cyber Security Tracking, Analysis and Response Center (CSTARC), tasked with conducting analysis of cyberspace threats and vulnerabilities, issuing alerts and warnings for cyberthreats, improving information sharing, responding to major cybersecurity incidents, and aiding in national-level recovery efforts.[80] In addition, a new Cyber Warning and Information Network (CWIN) has begun operation in 50 locations, and serves as an early warning system for cyberattacks.[81] The CWIN is engineered to be reliable and survivable, has no dependency on the Internet or the public switched network (PSN), and reportedly will not be affected if either the Internet or PSN suffer disruptions.[82]

In January 2004, the NCSD also created the National Cyber Alert System (NCAS), a coordinated national cybersecurity system that distributes information to subscribers to help identify, analyze, and prioritize emerging vulnerabilities and cyberthreats. NCAS is managed by the United States Computer Emergency Readiness Team (US-CERT), a partnership between NCSD and the private sector, and subscribers can sign up to receive notices from this new service by visiting the US-CERT website.[83]

However, despite growing concerns for national security, computer vulnerabilities persist, the number of computer attacks reported by industry and government has increased yearly, and federal agencies have, for the past three years, come under criticism for the poor effectiveness of their computer security programs.[84] For example, weaknesses in computer security at the Department of Energy reportedly allowed hackers to successfully penetrate systems 199 times in FY2004, affecting approximately 3,531 unclassified networked systems.[85] A report by the DOE inspector general stated that the Department continues to have difficulty finding, tracking and fixing previously reported cybersecurity weaknesses quickly. The report identified a number of other security weaknesses, and recommended that all major applications and general support systems become certified and accredited, according to DOE computer security policy.[86]

Chapter 3

ISSUES FOR CONGRESS

GROWING TECHNICAL CAPABILITIES OF TERRORISTS

Is it likely that the threat will increase in the future for a coordinated cyberattack, or other type of attack against computers that operate the U.S. infrastructure? As computer-literate youth increasingly join the ranks of terrorist groups, will cyberterrorism become increasingly more mainstream in the future? Will a computer-literate leader bring increased awareness of the advantages of an attack on information systems, or be more receptive to suggestions from other, newer computer-literate members? Once a new tactic has won widespread media attention, will it likely motivate other rival terrorist groups to follow along the new pathway.[87]

Several experts have asserted that terrorist organizations may soon begin to use computer technology to more actively support terrorist objectives. For example, seized computers belonging to Al Qaeda indicate its members are now becoming familiar with hacker tools that are freely available over the Internet. [88] Potentially severe cyberattack tools may be first developed and then secretly tested by dispersed terrorist groups using small, isolated laboratory networks, thus avoiding detection of any preparation before launching a widespread attack on the Internet.[89]

HOW BEST TO MEASURE CYBERATTACK TRENDS?

Congress may wish to encourage security and technology experts to study ways to collect data that will enable more effective analysis of trends of ongoing cyberattacks on the Internet. Currently, there is no published data to either support or deny terrorist involvement in the increasing number of cyberattacks that plague the Internet. Congress may wish to encourage researchers to find better ways to determine the initiators of cyberattacks.

What effects are new cyberattack tools, such as automated "bot" systems, having on the stability of the Internet infrastructure, and the security of the U.S. critical infrastructure?

Is there a need for a more statistically reliable analysis of trends in computer security vulnerabilities to more accurately show the costs and benefits for improving national cybersecurity? Currently, several annual studies are published by several security companies, analyzing what they have observed from customer monitoring or surveys. These reported statistics are relied upon for measuring financial losses to U.S. industry due to computer attacks. However, it is believed by some observers that some studies may be limited in scope and may possibly contain statistical bias.[90]

As technology evolves, will new and more innovative self-directed high technology products change the nature of our vulnerability to cyberattack? Currently, the degree and immediacy of human oversight of infrastructure computers will likely help prevent the effects of a possible cyberattack from cascading unpredictably. However, as more high technology products are designed to communicate directly with each other without human involvement, will the immediate oversight of human experts diminish, and would this also reduce our protection against a potentially severe cyberattack in the future?

DOD AND CYBERTERRORISM

In February 2003, the Administration published a report titled "National Strategy to Secure Cyberspace," making clear that the U.S. government reserves the right to respond "in an appropriate manner" if the United States comes under computer attack. The response could involve the use of U.S. cyberweapons, or malicious code designed to attack and disrupt the targeted computer systems of an adversary.

The Joint Information Operations Center (JIOC), which is under the U.S. Strategic Command (USSTRATCOM), has responsibility for managing information warfare and electronic warfare activities. Within the JIOC, the Joint Task Force-Global Network Operations (JTF-GNO), coordinates and directs the defense of DOD computer systems and networks, and, when directed, conducts computer network attack in support of combatant commanders' and national objectives.

Existing Guidance

The Bush Administration announced plans in February 2003 to develop national-level guidance for determining when and how the United States would launch computer network attacks against foreign adversary computer systems.[91] However, any U.S. response to a computer attack by an adversary must be carefully weighed to avoid mistakes in retaliation, or other possible unintended outcomes. Options for a cyberresponse from the United States may be limited because there will likely be difficulty in determining, with a high degree of certainty, if a terrorist group is actually responsible for an attack against computers in the United States. For example, a terrorist group might possibly subvert the computers of a third party, in an attempt to provoke a retaliatory strike by the United States against the wrong group or nation.

Retaliation

If it is determined that the United States has been the target of a successful coordinated cyberattack by a terrorist group, what is the appropriate response? There are many questions that can be raised regarding the military use of cyberweapons. For instance, should those decisions be made by the President, or by the Joint Chiefs of Staff, or by other military commanders? What oversight role should Congress have? Would the resulting effects of offensive cyberweapons for information warfare operations be difficult to limit or control? If the United States should use DOD cyberweapons to retaliate against a terrorist group, would that possibly encourage others to start launching cyberattacks against the United States? Similarly, will any U.S. attempt to suddenly increase surveillance via use of cyberespionage programs be labeled as an unprovoked attack, even if directed against a terrorist group? If a terrorist group should subsequently copy, or reverse-engineer a destructive U.S. military computer attack program, would it be used against other countries that are U.S. allies, or even turned back to attack civilian computer systems in the United States?[92] Would the use of cyberweapons, if the effects are widespread and severe, exceed the customary rules of military conflict, or international laws.[93]

In a meeting held in January 2003 at the Massachusetts Institute of Technology, White House officials sought input from experts outside government on guidelines for U.S. use of cyberweapons. Officials have stated they are proceeding cautiously, because a U.S. cyberattack against terrorist groups or other adversaries could have serious cascading effects, perhaps causing major disruption to civilian systems in addition to the intended computer targets.[94]

Military Vulnerability and Reliance on Commercial Products

Commercial electronics and communications equipment are now used extensively to support complex U.S. weapons systems, leaving operations for those systems possibly vulnerable to cyberattack, and this situation is known to our potential adversaries.[95] To what degree are military forces and national security threatened by vulnerabilities of commercial systems, and how can the computer industry be encouraged to create new COTS products that are less vulnerable to cyberattack?

PRIVACY

What is the proper balance between the need to detect and remain aware of terrorism activities and the need to protect individual privacy? Cyberterrorists would likely use tactics that are similar to those used by computer hacker groups. Preoperative surveillance characterizes the early stages of many cyberattacks, and secret planning may be conducted in Internet chat areas, where hackers meet anonymously to exchange information about computer vulnerabilities, or new cyberattack tools. These covert communications could also be encrypted and difficult to detect or decode.

A limiting factor for either preventing a cyberattack or identifying the attackers is a lack of data revealing evidence of pre-operative surveillance and on-line planning activity that is traceable back to terrorist groups. Should intelligence agencies monitor computer chat rooms frequented by terrorists and develop other ways to help uncover their communications and planning? Data Mining search technologies may offer ways to help the intelligence community uncover these linkages.

Terrorism Information Awareness Program

The Defense Advanced Research Projects Agency (DARPA) has conducted research and development for systems such as the former Terrorism Information Awareness Program (TIA)[96] that are intended to help investigators discover covert linkages among people, places, things, and events related to possible terrorist activity (see below for privacy issues). Funding ended for the TIA program in 2004 and the Information Awareness Office, a branch of DARPA, is now disbanded.[97] The TIA data mining program was intended to sift through vast quantities of citizens' personal data, such as credit card transactions and travel bookings, to identify possible terrorist activity to provide better advance information about terrorist planning and preparation activities to prevent future international terrorist attacks against the United States at home or abroad. However, the TIA program and other similar proposals for domestic surveillance raised privacy concerns from lawmakers, advocacy groups, and the media. Some privacy advocates have objected to the possibility that information gathered through domestic surveillance may be viewed by unauthorized users, or even misused by authorized users. Congress has moved to restrict or eliminate funding for the TIA program under S. 1382 and H.R. 2658.

P.L. 108-87, titled the Defense Appropriations Act of 2004, enacted on September 30, 2003, restricts funding and deployment of the TIA Program. Specifically, section 8131 part (a) limits use of funds for research and development of the TIA Program, except for "Processing, analysis, and collaboration tools for counterterrorism foreign intelligence" for military operations outside the United States.

Other Data Mining Search Technologies

Should more research be encouraged into newer database search technologies that provide more protection for individual privacy while helping to detect terrorist activities? The Department of Defense is currently reviewing the capabilities of other data mining products using technology that may reduce domestic privacy concerns raised by TIA. For example, Systems Research and Development, a technology firm based in Las Vegas, has been tasked by the CIA and other agencies to develop a new database search product called "Anonymous Entity Resolution." The technology used in this product can help investigators determine whether a terrorist suspect appears in two separate databases, without revealing any private individual information. The product uses encryption to ensure that even if the scrambled records are intercepted, no private information can be extracted. Thus, terrorism watch lists and corporate databases could be securely compared online, without revealing private information.[98]

Also, the Florida police department has, since 2001, operated a counter terrorism system called the Multistate Anti-Terrorism Information Exchange (MATRIX) that helps investigators find patterns among people and events by combining police records with commercially available information about most U.S. adults. MATRIX includes information that has always been available to investigators, but adds extraordinary processing speed. The Justice Department has provided $4 million to expand the MATRIX program nationally. DHS has pledged $8 million to assist with the national expansion, and has also announced plans to launch a pilot data-sharing network that will include Virginia, Maryland, Pennsylvania, and New York.[99]

For more information about TIA, data mining technology, and other privacy issues, see related CRS Reports.[100]

NATIONAL DIRECTOR FOR CYBERSECURITY

Each of the three top officials involved in the government's cybersecurity effort has resigned since the beginning of 2003. In January 2003, Richard Clarke resigned from his position as cybersecurity adviser to the President, ending a 30-year government career. Clarke had been the cybersecurity adviser since October 2001. Three months later, in April 2003, Howard Schmidt, Clarke's successor as adviser, resigned, ending a 31-year government career. Before becoming the adviser in January 2003, Schmidt had served as Clarke's deputy.

In September 2003, DHS formally announced the appointment of Amit Yoran as new director of its cybersecurity division.[101] However, the new director's position was placed three levels beneath DHS Secretary Tom Ridge, in contrast to Yoran's predecessors, Howard Schmidt and Richard Clarke, both of whom were positioned in the White House and had a direct line of contact with the President. In September 2004, Amit Yoran, resigned, citing the end of his one-year commitment to DHS. However, to some observers Yoran's resignation was unexpected.

Potential questions for Congress arising out of these resignations include the following: Were any of their resignations motivated in part by job-related concerns? If the latter, are these concerns indicative of any problems in the government's cybersecurity effort that need to be addressed? Why is the executive branch having difficulty holding onto senior cybersecurity officials? What effect has these resignations had on the government's efforts in cybersecurity? Are the government's efforts in this area suffering due to insufficient continuity of leadership?

The level of influence for the director of cybersecurity position has become a subject of recent debate, where several observers have proposed strengthening the director's position by moving it out of DHS and into the White House, possibly under the Office of Management and Budget. However, some security industry leaders have favored elevating the position to the assistant secretary level within DHS, and have objected to moving the position to another department, saying that relocating the office now would possibly be disruptive to the government-industry relationships that are newly formed at DHS.[102] DHS officials have reportedly resisted elevating the position, arguing that separating concerns for cybersecurity from physical security is inefficient and expensive because common problems threaten both.[103] P.L. 108-458, the Intelligence Reform and Terrorism Prevention Act, enacted on December 17, 2004, does not describe a new Assistant Secretary position for Cybersecurity.

H.R. 285 was introduced on January 6, 2005 by Representative Mac Thornberry, with Representative Zoe Lofgren and Representative Bennie Thompson as co-sponsors. This bill proposes to create a National Cybersecurity Office headed by an Assistant Secretary for Cybersecurity within the DHS Directorate for Information Analysis and Infrastructure Protection, with authority for all cybersecurity-related critical infrastructure protection programs. On February 18, 2005, the bill was referred to the House subcommittee on Economic Security, infrastructure Protection, and Cybersecurity.

SHOULD PHYSICAL AND CYBERSECURITY ISSUES REMAIN COMBINED?

According to news sources, in the 1980s during the Cold War, the United States CIA deliberately created faulty SCADA software and then planted it in locations where agents from the Soviet Union would steal it. Unknown to the Soviets, the SCADA software, which was supposedly designed to automate controls for gas pipelines, was also infected with a secret Trojan Horse programmed to reset pump speeds and valve settings that would create pressures far beyond what was acceptable to pipeline joints and welds. The result, in June 1982, was a monumental nonnuclear explosion on the trans-Siberian gas pipeline, equivalent to 3 kilotons of TNT. However, the event remained secret because the explosion took place in the Siberian wilderness, and there were no known casualties.[104]

DHS officials maintain that an attack against computers could possibly result in disastrous effects in physical facilities. Because of the this, the new DHS National Cyber Security Division (NCSD) is tasked to protect cyberassets in order to also provide the best protection for U.S. critical infrastructure assets. DHS officials have asserted that cybersecurity cuts across all aspects of critical infrastructure protection, and that cyberoperations cannot be separated from the physical aspects of businesses because they operate interdependently.[105] Therefore, the NCSD employs a threat-independent strategy of protecting the Internet and critical infrastructures from all types of attacks. DHS officials have stated, "If we attempt to "stovepipe" our protection efforts to focus on the different types of attackers who may use the cyberinfrastructure, we risk the possibility of limiting our understanding of the entire threat environment."[106]

However, officials of five business groups — the Cyber Security Industry Alliance, the Business Software Alliance, TechNet, the IT Association of America, and the Financial Services Roundtable — have urged the administration to create separate physical and cybersecurity reporting structures within the DHS. The industry groups maintain that the challenges of protection in a globally networked cyberworld are sufficiently different from requirements for protection in the physical world that DHS needs a separate structure; one that is focused on cyberissues, and headed by a Senate-confirmed public official.[107]

NATIONAL STRATEGY TO SECURE CYBERSPACE

Does the National Strategy to Secure Cyberspace present clear incentives for achieving security objectives? Suggestions to increase incentives may include requiring that all software procured for federal agencies be certified under the "Common Criteria" testing program, which is now the requirement for the procurement of military software. However, industry observers point out that the software certification process is lengthy and may interfere with innovation and competitiveness in the global software market.[108]

Should the National Strategy to Secure Cyberspace rely on voluntary action on the part of private firms, home users, universities, and government agencies to keep their networks secure, or is there a need for possible regulation to ensure best security practices? Has public response to improve computer security been slow partly because there are no regulations currently imposed?[109] Would regulation to improve computer security interfere with innovation and possibly harm U.S. competitiveness in technology markets? Two of the former cybersecurity advisers to the president have differing views: Howard Schmidt has stated that market forces, rather than the government, should determine how product technology should evolve for better cybersecurity; however, Richard Clarke has stated that the IT industry has done little on its own to improve security of its own systems and products.[110]

COMMERCIAL SOFTWARE VULNERABILITIES

Should software product vendors be required to create higher quality software products that are more secure and that need fewer patches? Software vendors may increase the level of security for their products by rethinking the design, or by adding more test procedures during product development. However, some vendors reportedly have said that their commercial customers may not be willing to pay the increased costs for additional security features.[111]

AWARENESS AND EDUCATION

Should computer security training be made available to all computer users to keep them aware of constantly changing computer security threats, and to encourage them to follow proper security procedures? A 2004 survey done by the National Cyber Security Alliance and AOL showed that home PC users had a low level of awareness about best practices for computer security. The survey showed that most home users do not have adequate protection against hackers, do not have updated antivirus software protection, and are confused about the protections they are supposed to use and how to use them.[112]

Will incentives, education programs, or public awareness messages about computer security encourage home PC users to follow the best security practices? Many computers taken over by Internet hackers belong to small businesses or individual home users who have not had training in best computer security practices and who may not feel motivated to voluntarily participate in a training program. Vulnerabilities that require government and corporate systems administrators to install software patches also affect computers belonging to millions of home PC users.[113]

COORDINATION TO PROTECT AGAINST CYBERTERRORISM

What can be done to improve sharing of information between federal government, local governments, and the private sector to improve computer security? Effective cybersecurity requires sharing of relevant information about threats, vulnerabilities, and exploits. A recent GAO survey of local government officials recommended that DHS strengthen information sharing by incorporating states and cities into its federal "enterprise architecture" planning process.[114] How can the private sector obtain useful information from the government on specific threats which the government considers classified, and how can the government obtain specific information from private industry about vulnerabilities and incidents which companies say they want to protect to avoid publicity and to guard trade secrets?[115]

Information Sharing

Should information voluntarily shared with the federal government about security vulnerabilities be shielded from disclosure through Freedom of Information Act requests? Many firms are reluctant to share important computer security information with government agencies because of the possibility of having competitors become aware of a company's security vulnerabilities through FOIA.

International Cooperation Against Cyberattack

How can the United States better coordinate security policies and international law to gain the cooperation of other nations to better protect against a computer attack? Pursuit of hackers may involve a trace back through networks requiring the cooperation of many Internet Service Providers located in several different nations.[116] Pursuit is made increasingly complex if one or more of the nations involved has a legal policy or political ideology that conflicts with that of the United States.[117]

Methods for improving international cooperation in dealing with cybercrime and terrorism were the subject of a conference sponsored by the Hoover Institution, the Consortium for Research on Information Security and Policy (CRISP) and the Center for International Security and Cooperation (CISAC) at Stanford University in 1999. Members of government, industry, NGOs, and academia from many nations met at Stanford to discuss the growing problem, and a clear consensus emerged that greater international cooperation is required.[118]

Currently, thirty-eight countries, including the United States, have signed the Council of Europe's Convention on Cybercrime, published in November 2001. The Convention seeks to better combat cybercrime by harmonizing national laws, improving investigative abilities, and boosting international cooperation. Supporters argue that the Convention will enhance deterrence, while critics counter it will have little effect without participation by countries in which cybercriminals operate freely. (see CRS Report RS21208, *Cybercrime: The Council of Europe Convention*).

Offshore Development of Software

Is U.S. national security threatened by using commercial software products developed in foreign countries.[119] A recent study by Gartner Inc., a technology research organization, predicts that for 2004 and beyond, more than 80 percent of U.S. companies will consider outsourcing critical IT services, including software development. Terrorist networks are known to exist in several countries such as Malaysia and Indonesia, where IT contract work has been outsourced. Other possible recipients of outsourced projects are Israel, India, Pakistan, Russia and China.[120] Corporations justify their actions by explaining that global economic competition makes offshore outsourcing a business necessity. Other observers point out that restricting offshore development may not be effective for improving national security because many foreign workers are also currently employed by domestic firms to develop computer software within the United States.

Chapter 4

LEGISLATIVE ACTIVITY

The Cybersecurity Research and Development Act (P.L. 107-305), authorized $903 million over five years for new research and training programs by the National Science Foundation (NSF) and the National Institute for Standards and Technology (NIST) to prevent and respond to terrorist attacks on private and government computers.

Following the September 11, 2001 attacks, the Federal Information Security Management Act (FISMA) of 2002 was enacted giving responsibility for setting security standards for civilian federal agency computer systems to the Office of Management and Budget (OMB).[121] Responsibility for security standards for national defense systems remains primarily with DOD and NSA.

The following bills identify recent legislative activity that is related to prevention of cyberterrorism, or related to collection of information on possible terrorist activities.

- **P.L. 108-195**: On December 19, 2003, the Defense Production Act of 2003 amended the Defense Production Act of 1950 to extend its expiration date and authorization of appropriations through FY2008. Sponsored by Senator Shelby Richard, this law corrects industrial resource shortfalls for radiation-hardened electronics, and defines "critical infrastructure" to include physical and cyberbased assets.
- ***S. 140**: Known as the Domestic Defense Fund Act of 2005, this bill proposes to authorize DHS to award grants to states and local governments to improve cyber and infrastructure security. Introduced by Senator Hillary Clinton on January 24, 2005, the bill was referred to the Senate Committee on Homeland Security and Governmental Affairs.

PLANNING FOR A CYBERATTACK

A cyberattack is sometimes also called a Computer Network Attack (CNA), because a network connection enables this type of attack. Computer hackers traditionally use five basic steps to gain unauthorized access, and subsequently take over computer systems. These five steps can also be employed by terrorist groups. The steps are frequently automated through use of special hacker tools freely available to anyone via the Internet.[122] Highly-skilled hackers use automated tools that are also very sophisticated, and their effects are initially much more difficult for computer security staff and security technology products to detect. These sophisticated hacker tools are usually shared only among an exclusive group of other highly-skilled hacker associates. The hacker tactics described in this report are also explained in detail in many sources that list possible defenses against computer attack.[123]

- **Step 1. Reconnaissance and Pre-operative Surveillance**
  In this first step, hackers employ extensive pre-operative surveillance to find out detailed information about an organization that will help them later gain unauthorized access to computer systems. The most common method is social engineering, or tricking an employee into revealing sensitive information (such as a telephone number or a password). Other methods include dumpster diving, or rifling through an organization's trash to find sensitive information (such as floppy disks or important documents that have not been shredded). This step can be automated if the attacker installs on an office computer a virus, worm, or "Spyware" program that performs surveillance and then transmits useful information, such as passwords, back to the attacker. "Spyware" is a form of malicious

code that is quietly installed on a computer without user knowledge when a user visits a malicious website. It may remain undetected by firewalls or current anti-virus security products while monitoring keystrokes to record web activity or collect snapshots of screen displays and other restricted information for transmission back to an unknown third party.[124]

- **Step 2. Scanning**
  Once in possession of special restricted information, or a few critical phone numbers, an attacker performs additional surveillance by scanning an organization's computer software and network configuration to find possible entry points. This process goes slowly, sometimes lasting months, as the attacker looks for several vulnerable openings into a system.[125]

- **Step 3: Gaining Access**
  Once the attacker has developed an inventory of software and configuration vulnerabilities on a target network, he or she may quietly take over a system and network by using a stolen password to create a phony account, or by exploiting a vulnerability that allows them to install a malicious Trojan Horse, or automatic "bot" that will await further commands sent through the Internet.

- **Step 4: Maintaining Access**
  Once an attacker has gained unauthorized access, he or she may secretly install extra malicious programs that allow them to return as often as they wish. These programs, known as "Root Kits" or "Back Doors", run unnoticed and can allow an attacker to secretly access a network at will. If the attacker can gain all the special privileges of a system administrator, then the computer or network has been completely taken over, and is "owned" by the attacker. Sometimes the attacker will reconfigure a computer system, or install software patches to close the previous security vulnerabilities just to keep other hackers out.

- **Step 5: Covering Tracks**
  Sophisticated attackers desire quiet, unimpeded access to the computer systems and data they take over. They must stay hidden to maintain control and gather more intelligence, or to refine preparations to maximize damage. The "Root Kit" or "Trojan Horse" programs often allow the attacker to modify the log files of the computer system, or to create hidden files to help avoid detection by the legitimate system administrator. Security systems may not detect the unauthorized activities of a careful intruder for a long period of time.[126]

As technology has evolved, more of the above tasks are now aided by the use of automated programs, or "bots," that are increasingly autonomous, rapid, and difficult to detect. These "bots" can be remotely controlled by commands sent through the Internet and can be activated to operate in a coordinated manner on thousands of computers in different locations around the world. Thousands of such computers under remote control may be programmed by a hacker to simultaneously launch an attack through the Internet that can be described as a "swarm."

CHARACTERISTICS OF MALICIOUS CODE

Technology constantly evolves, and new security vulnerabilities are discovered regularly by software vendors, by security organizations, by individual researchers, and often by computer hacker groups.[127] Security organizations, such as the Computer Emergency Response Team (CERT/CC) located at Carnegie Mellon, publish security advisories, including information about new software patches, usually before computer hacker groups can take advantage of newly discovered computer security vulnerabilities for purposes of cybercrime or cyberespionage. However, the number of reported unauthorized computer intrusions has increased every year, with a 56 percent increase reported between 2001 and 2002.[128]

Currently, many cyberattacks are enabled by "infecting" a computer with a malicious payload program that corrupts data, performs surveillance, or that receives commands through the Internet to paralyze or deny service to a targeted computer. A computer may become "infected" if a computer user mistakenly downloads and installs a malicious program, or mistakenly opens an infected email attachment. Other malicious programs, known as "worms," may actively and rapidly seek out other computers on the Internet having a specific non-patched vulnerability and automatically install themselves without any action required on the part of the victim.[129]

A virus is one form of malicious program that often immediately corrupts data or causes a malfunction. A Trojan Horse is another form of malicious program that quietly and secretly corrupts the functions of an existing trusted program on the computer. An attack program, once installed, may quietly "listen" for a special command sent through the Internet from a remote source, instructing it to begin activation of malicious program instructions. Another type of malicious program, known as "spyware," has a surveillance or espionage capability that enables it to secretly record and automatically transmit keystrokes and other information (including passwords) back to a remote attacker.[130] Other types of malicious code may combine some or all of the characteristics of viruses, worms, Trojan Horses, or spyware along with the ability to randomly change the electronic appearance (polymorphism) of the resulting attack code. This ability to change makes many of the newer viruses, worms, and Trojan Horses very difficult for most anti-virus security products to detect.[131]

Malicious programs attack by disrupting normal computer functions or by opening a back door for a remote attacker to take control of the computer. Sometimes an attacker can quietly take full control of a computer with the owner remaining unaware that his or her machine is compromised. An attack can either immediately disable a computer or incorporate a time delay, after which a remote command will direct the infected computer to transmit harmful signals that disrupt other computers. An attack can trigger the automatic transmission of huge volumes of harmful signals that can very rapidly disrupt or paralyze many thousands of other computers throughout the Internet or severely clog transmission lines with an abundance of bogus messages, causing portions of the Internet to become slow and unresponsive.

Preparation for a cybercrime or computer attack may sometimes proceed slowly or in several phases before a final attack is initiated. Some compromised computers become part of an automatic "bot network," quietly performing espionage by transmitting data or intermediate preparatory instructions back and forth between compromised computers while awaiting a special final activation signal originating from the attacker. The final activation phase may direct all compromised computers to inundate a targeted computer with bogus messages or insert phony data into critical computer systems, causing them to malfunction at a crucial point or affect other computers downstream. Some recent computer attacks have focused on only a single new computer vulnerability and have been seen to spread worldwide through the Internet with astonishing speed. [132]

The "Slammer" worm attacked Microsoft's database software and spread through the Internet over one weekend in January 2003. According to a preliminary study coordinated by the Cooperative Association for Internet Data Analysis (CAIDA), on January 25, 2003, the SQL Slammer worm (also known as "Sapphire") infected more than 90 percent of vulnerable computers worldwide within 10 minutes of its release on the Internet, making it the fastest computer worm in history. As the study reports, exploiting a known vulnerability for which a patch has been available since July 2002, Slammer doubled in size every 8.5 seconds and achieved its full scanning rate (55 million scans per second) after about 3 minutes. It caused considerable harm through network outages and such unforeseen consequences as canceled airline flights and automated teller machine (ATM) failures. Further, the study emphasizes that the effects would likely have been more severe had Slammer carried a malicious payload, attacked a more widespread vulnerability, or targeted a more popular service. The malicious code disrupted more than 13,000 Bank of America automated teller machines, causing some machines to stop issuing money, and took most of South Korea Internet users offline. As many as five of the 13 Internet root name servers were also slowed or disabled, according to Anti-virus firm F-Secure. Robert F. Dacey, "INFORMATION SECURITY: Progress Made, But Challenges Remain to Protect Federal Systems and the Nation's Critical Infrastructures," 2003; Matt Loney, "Slammer attacks may become way of life for Net ," *Cnet.News.com,* Feb. 6, 2003, [http://news.com.com/ Damage+control/2009-1001_3-983540.html]; Robert Lemos, "Worm exposes apathy, Microsoft flaws," Cnet.News.com, Jan. 26, 2003 [http://news.com.com/2102-1001-982135.html].

Appendix C

SIMILARITIES IN TACTICS USED FOR CYBERATTACKS AND CONVENTIONAL TERRORIST ATTACKS

Similarities exist in characteristics of tactics used by hackers to prepare for and execute a cybercrime or cyberespionage computer attack, and the tactics used by terrorists to prepare for and execute some recent physical terrorist operations. For example, both sets of tactics involve (1) network meetings in cyberspace, (2) extensive pre-attack surveillance, (3) exploits of soft and vulnerable targets, and (4) swarming methods. Knowing that these similarities exist may help investigators as they explore different methods to detect and prevent a possible cyberattack by terrorist groups:

- The organizational structures of many terrorist groups are not well understood and are usually intended to conceal the interconnections and relationships.[133] A network organization structure (as opposed to a hierarchical structure) favors smaller units, giving the group the ability to attack and quickly overwhelm defenders, and then just as quickly disperse or disappear. Terrorist groups using a network structure to plan and execute an attack can place government hierarchies at a disadvantage because a terrorist attack often blurs the traditional lines of authority between agencies such as police, the military, and other responders. Similarly, computer hackers are often composed of small groups or individuals who meet anonymously in network chat rooms to exchange information about computer vulnerabilities, and plan ways to exploit them for cybercrime or cyberespionage. By meeting only in cyberspace, hackers can quickly disappear whenever government authorities try to locate them.

- Terrorists use pre-attack surveillance over extended periods to gather information on a target's current patterns. According to news reports, Al Qaeda terrorists are now operating through "sleeper cells" scattered throughout the United States that are currently conducting pre-attack surveillance and relaying messages from terrorist leaders and planners.[134] Recent terrorist attacks on Westerners in Riyadh, Saudi Arabia in 2004 were reported to have involved extensive planning and preparation and were likely preceded by pre-attack surveillance.[135] Appendix A of this report describes how hackers engage in similar pre-operative surveillance activities before launching a cyberattack.

- Terrorist groups are described by DHS as opportunistic, choosing to exploit soft vulnerabilities that are left exposed. Similarly, an increasingly popular trend for computer hackers engaged in computer crime or computer espionage is to use a malicious program called a worm, that pro-actively spreads copies of itself through the Internet, rapidly finding as many computers as possible with the same non-patched vulnerability, and then automatically installing itself to quietly await further instructions from the attacker.

- Hackers have also designed recent computer exploits that launch anonymously from thousands of infected computers to produce waves of disruption that can quickly overwhelm a targeted organization, or multiple organizations such as a list of banking institutions. In a similar manner, terrorist groups may also strike in waves from multiple dispersed directions against multiple targets, in swarming campaigns. An example of swarming may be the May 11, 2003 attack in Riyadh, where terrorists (possibly Al Qaeda), staged simultaneous assaults at three compounds in different locations, with each assault involving a rapid strike with multiple vehicles, some carrying explosives and others carrying gunmen. Another example may be the simultaneous attacks of 9/11 which were directed against the towers of the World Trade Center, the Pentagon, and a possible third target.

ENDNOTES

[1] For example, enemy fighters in Iraq have reportedly employed a strategy of directing a large portion of their attacks against U.S. rear guard and support units. Christopher Cooper, "Black Recruits Slide As Share of Army Forces," *Wall Street Journal*, Oct. 7, 2004, p. B1.

[2] Dan Kuehl, professor at the National Defense University School of Information Warfare and Strategy, has pointed out that a high percentage of U.S. military messages flow through commercial communications channels, and this reliance creates a vulnerability during conflict.

[3] The critical infrastructure is viewed by some as more resilient than previously thought to the effects of a computer attack. Drew Clark, "Computer Security Officials Discount Chances of 'Digital Pearl Harbor,'" June 3, 2003, [http://www.GovExec.com].

[4] Joshua Green, "The Myth of Cyberterrorism," *Washington Monthly*, Nov. 2002, [*http://www.amazon.com/exec/obidos/external-search/104-9945259-0829500?keyword=The+Myth+of+Cyberterrorism&mode =blended&tag=thewashington-20&Go.x=14&Go.y =14*].

[5] All methods of computer attack are within the current capabilities of several nations. See CRS Report RL31787, *Information Warfare and Cyberwar: Capabilities and Related Policy Issues*.

[6] Advantages of EA and CNA might derive from United States reliance on a computer-controlled critical infrastructure, along with unpredict-able results depending on severity of the attack. Jason Sherman, "Bracing for Modern Brands of Warfare," *Air Force Times*, Sept. 27, 2004, [*http://www.airforcetimes.com/story.php?f=1AIRPAPER-358 727.php*].

[7] Steven Marlin and Martin Garvey, "Disaster-Recovery Spending on the Rise," *Information Week*, Aug. 9, 2004, p.26.

[8]   For more on conventional, chemical, nuclear, and biological terrorism, see
        CRS Report RL30153, *Critical Infrastructures: Background, Policy, and
        Implementation*; CRS Report RL31669, *Terrorism: Background on
        Chemical, Biological, and Toxin Weapons and Options for Lessening Their
        Impact*; CRS Report RL32595, *Nuclear Terrorism: A Brief Review of
        Threats and Responses*; and CRS Issue Brief IB10119, *Terrorism and
        National Security: Issues and Trends*.

[9]   Electrical systems connected to any wire or line that can act as an antenna
        may   be   disrupted.   [*http://www.physics.northwestern.edu/
        classes/2001Fall/Phyx135-2/19/emp.htm*]. "Maintenance of Mechani-cal
        and Electrical Equipment at Command, Control, Communications,
        Computers, Intelligence, Surveillance, and Reconnaissance (C4ISR)
        Facilities," *HEMP Protection Systems*, Chapter 27, *Army Training Manual*
        5-692-2,   April   15,   2001   [*http://www.usace.army.mil
        /publications/armytm/tm5-692-2/chap27VOL-2.pdf*].

[10]   Kenneth R. Timmerman, "U.S. Threatened with EMP Attack," *Insight on
        the News*, May 28, 2001, [*http://www.insightmag.com/news/2001
        /05/28/InvestigativeReport/U.Threatened.With.Emp.Attack-210973. shtml*].

[11]   House Armed Services Committee, *Committee Hearing on Commission to
        Assess the Threat to the United States from Electro-magnetic Pulse Attack*,
        July 22, 2004. "Experts Cite Electromagnetic Pulse as Terrorist Threat," *Las
        Vegas Review-Journal*, Oct. 3, 2001.

[12]   Seth Schiesel, "Taking Aim at An Enemy's Chips," *New York Times*, Feb.
        20, 2003.

[13]   Michael Sirak, "U.S. Vulnerable to EMP Attack," *Jane's Defence Weekly*,
        July   26,   2004,   [*http://www.janes.com/defence/news/jdw/
        jdw040726_1_n.shtml*].

[14]   Dr. John Foster, Jr., et al., *Report of the Commission to Assess the Threat to
        the United States from Electromagnetic Pulse (EMP) Attack: Volume 1:
        Executive Report*, report to Congress, 2004. And, Daniel G. Dupont, "Panel
        Says Society At Great Risk From Electomagnetic Pulse Attack," *Inside the
        Pentagon*, July 15, 2004, p.1.

[15]   Statement of Dr. Peter M. Fonash, Acting Deputy Manager, National
        Communications System, Department of Homeland Security, before the
        U.S. Senate Judiciary Committee, Subcommittee on Terrorism, Technology,
        and Homeland Security, March 5, 2005.

[16]   While experts disagree about whether any terrorist organizations are capable
        of building an inexpensive electromagnetic pulse device, it may be possible
        to acquire a device from a terrorist-sponsoring nation. Michael Abrams,

"The Dawn of the E-Bomb," *IEEE Spectrum Online*, Nov. 2003, [*http://www.spectrum.ieee.org/WEBONLY/publicfeature/   nov03/ 1103ebom.html*].

[17] Some forms of EA are intended to overpower a radio transmission signal to block or "jam" it, while other forms of EA are intended to overpower a radio signal and replace it with a substitute signal that disrupts processing logic or stored data. David Fulghum, "Network Wars," *Aviation Week & Space Technology*, Oct. 25, 2004, p.91.

[18] The United States has employed this definition of terrorism for statistical and analytical purposes since 1983. U.S. Department of State, 2002, *Patterns of Global Terrorism,2003*, [*http://www.state.gov/ s/ct/rls/pgtrpt/2001/html/10220.htm*].

[19] [*http://www.fema.gov/pdf/onp/toolkit_app_d.pdf*].

[20] Dorothy Denning, "Activism, Hactivism, and Cyberterrorism: The Internet as a tool for Influencing Foreign Policy," in John Arquilla and David Ronfeldt, ed., *Networks and Netwars*, (Rand, 2001), p. 241.

[21] Serge Krasavin, *What is Cyberterrorism?*, Computer Crime Research Center, Apr. 23, 2004, [*http://www.crime-research.org/analytics/ Krasavin/*].

[22] Dorothy Denning, *Is Cyber War Next?*, Social Science Research Council, Nov. 2001, [*http://www.ssrc.org/sept11/essays/denning.htm*].

[23] Dan Verton, *A Definition of Cyber-terrorism*, Computerworld, Aug. 11, 2003, [*http://www.computerworld.com/securitytopics/security/ story/0,10801,83843,00.html*].

[24] DHS press release, "Ridge Creates New Division to Combat Cyber Threats," June 6, 2003, [*http://www.dhs.gov/dhspublic/display? content=916*].

[25] John Arquilla and David Ronfeldt, "The Advent of Netwar (Revisited)," *Networks and Netwars: The Future of Terror, Crime and Militancy*, (Santa Monica: Rand, 2001), pp. 1-28.

[26] An incident may involve one site or hundreds (or even thousands) of sites. Also, some incidents may involve ongoing activity for long per-iods of time. *The Computer Emergency Response Team Coordination Center (CERT/CC) Statistics 1988-2004*, [*http://www.cert.org/stats/ cert_stats.html*].

[27] Many cyberattacks are unreported usually because the organization is unable to recognize that it has been attacked, or because the organization is reluctant to reveal publicly that it has experienced a computer attack, Government Accountability Office, *Information Security: Further Efforts*

Needed to Fully Implement Statutory Requirements in DOD, GAO-03-1037T, July 24, 2003, p. 6.

[28] Symantec, *Symantec Internet Security Threat Report*, Feb.2003, p. 48.

[29] "The Myths and Facts behind Cyber Security Risks for Industrial Control Systems," *Proceedings of the ISA Expo 2004*, Houston, Texas, Oct. 5, 2004.

[30] Frank Tiboni, "DOD Plans Network Task Force," *FCW.com*, Sept. 28, 2004, [*http://www.fcw.com/fcw/articles/2004/0927/web-dod-09-28-04. asp*].

[31] James Lewis, "Assessing the Risks of Cyber Terrorism, Cyber War and Other Cyber Threats," Dec. 2002, [*http://www.csis.org/tech/0211_lewis.pdf*].

[32] At the annual conference of the Center for Conflict Studies, Phil Williams, Director of the Program on Terrorism and Trans-National Crime and the University of Pittsburgh, said an attack on the global financial system would likely focus on key nodes in the U.S. financial infrastructure: Fedwire and Fednet. Fedwire is the financial funds transfer system that exchanges money among U.S. banks, while Fednet is the electronic network that handles the transactions. The system has one primary installation and three backups. "You can find out on the Internet where the backups are. If those could be taken out by a mix of cyber and physical activities, the U.S. economy would basically come to a halt," Williams said. "If the takedown were to include the international funds transfer networks CHIPS and SWIFT then the entire global economy could be thrown into chaos." George Butters, "Expect Terrorist Attacks on Global Financial System," Oct. 10, 2003, [http://www.theregister. co.uk/content/55/33269.html].

[33] The simulation involved more than 100 participants. Gartner, Inc., "Cyberattacks: The Results of the Gartner/U.S. Naval War College Simulation," July, 2002, [http://www3.gartner.com/2_events /audioconferences/dph/dph.html.] War game participants were divided into cells, and devised attacks against the electrical power grid, telecommunications infrastructure, the Internet and the financial services sector. It was determined that "peer-to-peer networking", a special method of communicating where every PC used commonly available software to act as both a server and a client, posed a potentially critical threat to the Internet itself. William Jackson, "War College Calls Digital Pearl Harbor Doable," *Government Computer News*, Aug. 23, 2002, [http://www.gcn.com/vol1_no1/daily-updates/19792-1.html].

[34] The vulnerability was found in Abstract Syntax Notation One (ASN.1) encoding, and was extremely widespread. Ellen Messmer, "President's Advisor Predicts Cyber-catastrophes Unless Security Improves," *Network*

World Fusion, July 9, 2002, [http://www.nwfusion.com/news/2002/0709schmidt.html].

[35] Barton Gellman, "Cyber-Attacks by Al Qaeda Feared," *Washington Post*, June 27, 2002, p. A01.

[36] The most expensive natural disaster in U.S. history, Hurricane Andrew, is reported to have caused $25 billion dollars in damage, while the Love Bug virus is estimated to have cost computer users around the world somewhere between $3 billion and $15 billion. However, the Love Bug virus was created and launched by a single university student in the Philippines, relying on inexpensive computer equipment. Christopher Miller, *GAO Review of Weapon Systems Software*, Mar. 3, 2003, Email communication, MillerC@gao.gov.

[37] Congestion caused by the Blaster worm delayed the exchange of critical power grid control data across the public telecommunications network, which could have hampered the operators' ability to prevent the cascading effect of the blackout. Dan Verton, "Blaster Worm Linked to Severity of Blackout," *Computerworld*, Aug. 29, 2003, [http://www.computerworld.com/printthis/2003/0,4814,84510,00.html]

[38] Proprietary systems are unique, custom built software products intended for installation on a few (or a single) computers, and their uniqueness makes them a less attractive target for hackers. They are less attractive because finding a security vulnerability takes time (See Appendix A), and a hacker may usually not consider it worth their while to invest the preoperative surveillance and research needed to attack a proprietary system on a single computer. Widely used Commercial-Off-The-Shelf (COTS) software products, on the other hand, are more attractive to hackers because a single security vulnerability, once discovered in a COTS product, may be embedded in numerous computers that have the same COTS software product installed.

[39] Industrial computers sometimes have operating requirements that differ from business or office computers. For example, monitoring a chemical process, or a telephone microwave tower may require 24-hour continuous availability for a critical industrial computer. Even though industrial systems may operate using COTS software (see above), it may be economically difficult to justify suspending the operation of an industrial SCADA computer on a regular basis to take time to install every new security software patch. See interview with Michael Vatis, director of the Institute for Security Technology Studies related to counterterrorism and cybersecurity. Sharon Gaudin, "Security Expter: U.S. Companies

Unprepared for Cyber Terror," *Datamation*, July 19, 2002, [*http://itmanagement. earthweb.com/secu/ article.php/1429851*]. Also, Government Accountability Office, *Information Security: Further Efforts Needed to Fully Implement Statutory Requirements in DOD*, GAO-03-1037T, July 24, 2003, p. 8.

[40] Kevin Poulsen, "Slammer Worm Crashed Ohio Nuke Plant Network," *Security Focus*, Aug. 19, 2003, [*http://www.securityfocus.com /news/ 6767*].

[41] Scott Nance, "Debunking Fears: Exercise Finds 'Digital Pearl Harbor' Risk Small," *Defense Week*, Apr. 7, 2003, [*http://www.kingpublishing. com/publications/dw/*].

[42] Brigadier Gen. Dennis Moran, U.S. Central Command/ J6, in U.S. Congress, House Armed Services Subcommittee on Terrorism, Unconventional Threats and Capabilities, *Hearing on Military C4I Systems*, Oct. 21, 2003, [http://www.cq.com].

[43] Christopher Casteilli,"DOD and Thailand Run Classified 'Eligible Receiver' Info-War Exercise," *Defense Information and Electronics Report*, 2002, vol. 77, no. 44.

[44] Briefing on "Eligible Receiver 2003" by DOD staff for the Congressional Research Service, January 9, 2003.

[45] Some ships of the U.S. Navy use Windows software. Bill Murray, "Navy Carrier to Run Win 2000," *GCN.com*, Sept. 11, 2000, [http://www.gcn.com/vol19_no27/dod/2868-1.html]. Major U.K. naval systems defense contractor, BAE Systems, also took the decision to standardize future development on Microsoft Windows. John Lettice, "OSS Torpedoed: Royal Navy Will Run on Windows for Warships,"*Register*, Sept. 6, 2004, [*http://www.theregister.co.uk/ 2004/09/06/ams_goes_windows_for_warships/*].

[46] Patience Wait, "Defense IT Security Can't Rest on COTS," *GCN.com*, Sept. 27, 2004, [http://www.gcn.com/23_29/news/27422-1.html].

[47] Dawn Onley, "Army Urged to Step Up IT Security Focus," *GCN.com*, Sept.2, 2004, [http://www.gcn.com/vol1_no1/daily-updates/27138-1.html].

[48] Patience Wait, "Defense IT Security Can't Rest on COTS," *GCN.com*, Sept.27, 2004, [http://www.gcn.com/23_29/news/27422-1.html].

[49] "E-crime Watch Survey Shows Significant Increase in Electronic Crimes," *CSOonline.com*, May 25, 2004, [*http://www.csoonline.com/ releases/ecrimewatch04.pdf*].

[50] "Internet Worm Keeps Striking," January 27, 2003, *CBSNews.com*, [http://www.cbsnews.com/stories/2003/01/28/tech/main538200.shtml]

[51] "CERT/CC   Statistics   1988-2004,"   [*http://www.cert.org/stats/cert_
       stats.html*].

[52] The SANS Institute, in cooperation with the National Infrastructure
       Protection Center (NIPC), publishes an annual list of the 10 most commonly
       exploited vulnerabilities for Windows systems and for Unix systems. *The
       SANS/FBI Twenty Most Critical Internet Security Vulnerabilities, 2003*,
       SANS, Apr. 15, 2003 [*http://www. sans.org/top20/*].

[53] In September, 2003, Microsoft Corporation announced three new critical
       flaws in its latest Windows operating systems software. Security experts
       predicted that computer hackers may possibly exploit these new
       vulnerabilities by releasing more attack programs, such as the "Blaster
       worm" that recently targeted other Windows vulnerabilities causing
       widespread disruption on the Internet. Jaikumar Vijayan, "Attacks on New
       Windows Flaws Expected Soon," *Computerworld*, Sept. 15, 2003, vol. 37,
       no. 37, p. 1.

[54] Jonathan   Krim,   "Security   Report   Puts   Blame   on   Microsoft,"
       Washingtonpost.com, Sept. 24, 2003. Joshua Green, "The Myth of
       Cyberterrorism,"   *Washington   Monthly*,   Nov.   2002   [*http://www.
       washingtonmonthly.com/*].

[55] Agencies operating national security systems must purchase software
       products from a list of lab-tested and evaluated products in a program that
       requires vendors to submit software for review in an accredited lab, a
       process (known as certification and accreditation under the Common
       Criteria, a testing program run by the National Information Assurance
       Partnership) that often takes a year and costs several thousand dollars. The
       review requirement previously has been limited to military national security
       software, however, the administration has stated that the government will
       undertake a review of the program in 2003 to "possibly extend" it as a new
       requirement for civilian agencies. Ellen Messmer, White House issue
       "National Strategy to Secure Cyberspace," *Network World Fusion*, February
       14, 2003 [http://www.nwfusion.com/news/2003/0214ntlstrategy.html].

[56] Richard D. Pethia, Director, CERT/CC, Software Engineering Institute,
       Carnegie Mellon University, Testimony before the House Select Committee
       on Homeland Security, Subcommittee on Cybersecurity, Science, and
       Research and Development, *Overview of the Cyber Problem — A Nation
       Dependent and Dealing with Risk*, hearing, June 25, 2003,
       [*http://www.cert.org /congressional_ testimony/Pethia_testimony_06-25-
       03.html#factors*].

[57] Scott Charney, Chief Security Strategist, Microsoft, Statement before the House Committee on Armed Services, Terrorism, Unconventional Threats and Capabilities Subcommittee, *Information Technology in the 21st Century Battlespace*, hearing, July 24, 2003, p.9.

[58] A survey of 2000 PC users found that 42% had not downloaded the vendor patch to ward off the recent Blaster worm attack, 23% said they do not regularly download software updates, 21% do not update their anti-virus signatures, and 70% said they were not notified by their companies about the urgent threat due to the Blaster worm. Jaikumar Vijayan, "IT Managers Say They Are Being Worn Down by Wave of Attacks," *Computerworld*, Aug. 25, 2003, vol. 37, no. 34, P.1.

[59] According to security group Attrition.org, failure to keep software patches up to date resulted in 99 percent of 5,823 website defacements in 2003. Robert Lemos, "Software "Fixes" Routinely Available but Often Ignored," 2003 [http://news.com.com/2102-1017-251407.html] , and Richard D. Pethia, Director, CERT/CC, Software Engineering Institute, Carnegie Mellon University, Testimony before the House Select Committee on Homeland Security, Subcommittee on Cybersecurity, Science, and Research and Development, Hearing on *Overview of the Cyber Problem — A Nation Dependent and Dealing with Risk*, June 25, 2003 [*http://www.cert.org /congressional_ testimony/Pethia_testimony_06-25-03.html #factors*].

[60] Gartner Inc., a technology research organization, has estimated that by 2004, more than 80% of U.S. companies will have had high-level discussions about offshore outsourcing, and 40% will have completed a pilot program. Patrick Thibodeau, "Offshore's Rise Is Relentless," *Computerworld*, June 30, 2003, vol. 37, no. 26, p.1.

[61] Scott Charney, Chief Security Strategist, Microsoft, Statement before the House Committee on Armed Services, Terrorism, Unconventional Threats and Capabilities Subcommittee, *Information Technology in the 21st Century Battlespace*, hearing, July 24, 2003, p.11.

[62] The success of the Vehicle Borne Improvised Explosive Devices (VBIEDs) used in the May 11, 2003 terrorist attacks in Riyadh, likely depended on extensive advance surveillance of the multiple targets. Protective measures against such attacks rely largely on watching for signs of this pre-operational surveillance. Gary Harter, "Potential Indicators of Threats Involving VBIEDs," Homeland Security Bulletin, Risk Assessment Division, Information Analysis Directorate, DHS, May 15, 2003.

[63] Dorothy Denning, "Levels of Cyberterror Capability: Terrorists and the Internet," [http://www.cs.georgetown.edu/~denning/infosec /Denning-

Cyberterror-SRI.ppt]; presentation, and Zack Phillips, "Homeland Tech Shop Wants to Jump-Start Cybersecurity Ideas," *CQ Homeland Security*, September 14, 2004, [*http://homeland.cq.com/hs/ display.do?docid=1330150&sourcetype=31&binderName=news-all*].

[64] Report was published in 1999, available at [*http://www.nps.navy.mil/ ctiw/reports/*].

[65] The Ashland Institute for Strategic Studies has observed that Al Qaeda is more fixated on physical threats than electronic ones. John Swartz, "Cyberterror Impact, Defense Under Scrutiny," *USA Today*, Aug. 3, 2004, p. 2B.

[66] David Kaplan, "Playing Offense: The Inside Story of How U.S. Terrorist Hunters Are Going after Al Qaeda," *U.S. News & World Report*, June 2, 2003, pp. 19-29.

[67] Robert Windrem, "9/11 Detainee: Attack Scaled Back," Sept. 21, 2003, [http://www.msnbc.com/news/969759.asp].

[68] "Terrorism: An Introduction," April 4, 2003, [*http://www.terrorism answers.com/ terrorism*].

[69] James Lewis, "Assessing the Risks of Cyber Terrorism, Cyber War and Other Cyber Threats," Dec. 2002 [*http://www.csis.org/tech/ 0211_lewis.pdf*].

[70] In May2003, the President lifted all terrorism related sanctions that had been imposed on Iraq, taking it off the terrorism list, but only de facto. Libya is still on the list, although some sanctions have been eased. U.S. Department of State, *2003 Patterns of Global Terrorism Report*, April 29, 2004, [*http://www.state.gov/s/ct/rls/pgtrpt/2003/316 44.htm*].

[71] Riptech Internet Security Threat Report, *Attack Trends for Q1 and Q2 2002*, [*http://www.securitystats.com/reports/Riptech-Internet_Security _Threat_Report_vII.200 20708.pdf*]. (Riptech was purchased in 2002 by Symantec, Inc.)

[72] Kim Zetter, "Faux Cyberwar," *Computer Security*, May 2003, vol.6, no.5, p. 22.

[73] Brian McWilliams, "Iraq's Crash Course in Cyberwar," Wired News, May 22, 2003, [*http://www.wired.com/news/print/0,1294,58901,00. html*].

[74] Brian McWilliams,, "North Korea's School for Hackers," Wired News.com, June 2, 2003 [*http://www.wired.com/news/conflict/0,2100, 59043,00.html*].

[75] The civilian population of North Korea is reported to have a sparse number of computers, with only a few locations offering connections to the Internet, while South Korea is one of the most densely-wired countries in the world, with 70 percent of all households having broadband Internet access. During

the recent global attack involving the "Slammer" computer worm, many Internet service providers in South Korea were severely affected. "North Korea May be Training Hackers," *Miami Herald Online*, May 16, 2003, [*http://www.miami. com/mld/miamiherald/news/world/5877291.htm*].

[76] Dorothy Denning, "Cyber Terrorism," August 24, 2000, [*http://www.cs.georgetown.edu/~denning/infosec/cyberterrorGD.doc*].

[77] Hackers sell their information anonymously through secretive websites. Bob Francis, "Know Thy Hacker," *Infoworld* , J anuary 28, 2005, [*http://www.infoworld.com/article/05/01/28/05OPsecadvise_1. html*].

[78] GAO has noted that many federal agencies have not implemented security requirements for most of their systems, and must meet new requirements under FISMA. See GAO Report GAO-03-852T, *Information Security: Continued Efforts Needed to Fully Implement Statutory Requirements*, June 24, 2003.

[79] Tinabeth Burton, *ITAA Finds Much to Praise in National Cybersecurity Plan,* May 7, 2003, [*http://www.findarticles.com/p/ articles/mi_go1965/is_200303/ai_n7418485*]

[80] DHS is comprised of five major divisions or directorates: Border & Transportation Security; Emergency Preparedness & Response; Science & Technology; Information Analysis & Infrastructure Protection; and Management. See [*http://www.dhs.gov/dhspublic/dis play?theme=52*].

[81] Bara Vaida, "Warning Center for Cyber Attacks is Online, Official Says," *Daily Briefing*, GovExec.com, June 25, 2003.

[82] The Cyber Warning Information Network (CWIN) provides voice and data connectivity to government and industry participants in support of critical infrastructure protection, [*http://www.publicsectorinstitute.net /ELetters/HomelandSecurityStrategies/Volume1No1/CyberWarningNetLaun ch.lsp*] .

[83] [http://www.us-cert.gov/cas/].

[84] Based on 2002 data submitted by federal agencies to the White House Office of Management and Budget, GAO noted, in testimony before the House Committee on Government Reform (GAO-03-564T, April 8, 2003), that all 24 agencies continue to have "significant information security weaknesses that place a broad array of federal operations and assets at risk of fraud, misuse, and disruption.", Christopher Lee, "Agencies Fail Cyber Test: Report Notes 'Significant Weaknesses' in Computer Security," November 20, 2002 [*http://www.washington post.com/ac2/wp-dyn/A12321- 2002Nov19?language=printer*].

[85] Wilson Dizard, "DOE Hacked 199 Times Last Year," GCN.com, September 30, 2004, [http://www.gcn.com/vol1_no1/daily-updates/27489-1.html], and U.S. Department of Energy Office of Inspector General, *Office of Audit Operations Evaluation Report*, DOE/IG-0662, September, 2004, [*http://www.ig.doe.gov/pdf/ig-0662. pdf*].

[86] *Evaluation Report: The Department's Unclassified Cyber Security Program - 2004*, DOE/IG-0662, September 2004, [*http://www.ig.doe. gov/pdf/ig-0662.pdf*].

[87] Jerrold M. Post, Kevin G. Ruby, and Eric D. Shaw, "From Car Bombs to Logic Bombs: The Growing Threat From Information Terrorism," *Terrorism and Political Violence*, Summer 2000, vol.12, no.2, pp. 97-122.

[88] Richard Clarke, "Vulnerability: What Are Al Qaeda's Capabilities?" *PBS Frontline: Cyberwar*, April 2003, [*http://www.pbs.org*].

[89] Networking technologies, such as the Internet, are advantageous for attackers who are geographically dispersed. Networking supports redundancy within an organization, and it suggests the use of swarming tactics, new weapons, and other new strategies for conducting conflict that show advantages over traditional government hierarchies. Inflexibility is a major disadvantage when a hierarchy confronts a networked organization. Networks blend offensive and defensive functions, while hierarchies struggle with allocating responsibility for either. John Arquilla, David Ronfeldt, 2001, *Networks and Netwars*, (Santa Monica: Rand, 2001), p. 285.

[90] A well known source of information about the costs of cyberattacks is the annual computer security survey published by the Computer Security Institute (CSI), which utilizes data collected by the FBI. However, respondents to the CSI/FBI survey of computer security issues are generally limited only to CSI members, which may create statistical bias that affects the survey findings. Recently, CSI has also conceded weaknesses in its analytical approach and has suggested that its survey of computer security vulnerabilities and incidents may be more illustrative than systematic. However, the CSI/FBI survey remains useful despite its imperfect methodology. Bruce Berkowitz and Robert W. Hahn, "Cybersecurity: Who's Watching the Store?," *Issues in Science and Technology*, Spring 2003.

[91] The guidance, known as National Security Presidential Directive 16, was signed in July 2002 and is intended to clarify circumstances under which an

information warfare attack by DOD would be justified, and who has authority to launch a computer attack.

[92] See CRS Report RL31787, *Information Warfare and Cyberwar: Capabilities and Related Policy Issues*, by Clay Wilson.

[93] The laws of war are international rules that have evolved to resolve practical problems relating to military conflict, such as restraints to prevent misbehavior or atrocities, and have not been legislated by an overarching central authority. The United States is party to various limiting treaties. For example, innocent civilians are protected during war under the Convention on Prohibitions or Restrictions on the Use of Certain Conventional Weapons Which May Be Deemed to be Excessively Injurious or to have Indiscriminate Effects. Sometimes the introduction of new technology tends to force changes in the understanding of the laws of war. Gary Anderson and Adam Gifford, "Order Out of Anarchy: The International Law of War," *The Cato Journal*, vol. 15, no. 1, p. 25-36.

[94] Bradley Graham, "Bush Orders Guidelines for Cyber-Warfare," *Washington Post*, Feb. 7, 2003, p. 1.

[95] Stanley Jakubiak and Lowell Wood, "DOD Uses Commercial Software and Equipment in Tactical Weapons ," Statements before the House Military Research and Development Subcommittee, Hearing on EMP Threats to the U.S. Military and Civilian Infrastructure, October 7, 1999. House Armed Services Committee, *Commission to Assess the Threat to the United States from Electromagnetic Pulse Attack*, hearing,July 22, 2004.

[96] Funding for the controversial Terrorism Information Awareness program ended in 2004. The prototype system was formerly housed within the DARPA Information Awareness Office. Several related data mining research and development programs, now managed by different agencies, are designed to provide better advance information about terrorist planning and preparation activities to prevent future international terrorist attacks against the United States at home or abroad. A goal of data mining is to treat worldwide distributed database information as if it were housed within one centralized database. *Report to Congress Regarding the Terrorism Information Awareness Program*, Executive Summary, May 20 2003, p. 1.

[97] House and Senate conferees voted on September 24 to end funding for TIA through 2004. Steven M. Cherry, "Controversial Pentagon Program Scuttled, But Its Work Will Live On," *IEEE Spectrum Online*, Sept. 29, 2003, [http://www.spectrum.ieee.org].

[98] Pentagon sources familiar with the "Anonymous Entity Resolution" technology have indicated that it may alleviate some of the issues associated

with privacy protection. The product uses "entity-resolution techniques" to scramble data for security reasons. The software sifts through data such as names, phone numbers, addresses and information from employers to identify individuals listed under different names in separate databases. The software can find information by comparing records in multiple databases, however the information is scrambled using a "one-way hash function," which converts a record to a character string that serves as a unique identifier like a fingerprint. Persons being investigated remain anonymous, and agents can isolate particular records without examining any other personal information. A record that has been one-way hashed cannot be "un-hashed" to reveal information contained in the original record. Steve Mollman, "Betting on Private Data Search," *Wired.com*, Mar. 11, 2003.

[99] Robert O'Harrow, "U.S. Backs Florida's New Counterterrorism Database," *Washington Post*, Aug. 6, 2003, p. A01.

[100] CRS Report RL31786, *Total Information Awareness Programs: Funding, Composition, and Oversight Issues*, CRS Report RL31730, *Privacy: Total Information Awareness Programs and Related Information Access, Collection, and Protection Laws*, CRS Report RL31798, *Data Mining: An Overview*, and CRS Report RL31846, *Science and Technology Policy: Issues for the 108th Congress*, 2nd Session .

[101] The deputy director of the cybersecurity division, Andrew Purdy, has since been appointed interim director of U.S. cybersecurity.

[102] Dan Verton, "Update: Cybersecurity Overhaul Legislation DOA in Congress," *ComputerWorld*, Sept. 23, 2004, [*http://www.computer world.com/securitytopics /security/story/0,10801,96126,00.html*].

[103] The DHS cybersecurity center has five primary roles: conducting cybersecurity research; developing performance standards; fostering public-private sector communication; supporting the DHS information analysis and infrastructure protection directorate; and working with the National Science Foundation on educational programs, *Congress Daily AM*, May 15, 2003.

[104] NORAD monitors first suspected that the explosion was a nuclear explosion, but satellites did not pick up an electromagnetic pulse that would have accompanied a nuclear detonation. William Safire, "The Farewell Dossier," *New York Times*, Feb. 4, 2004, [*http://www. nytimes.com/2004/02/02/opinion/02SAFI.html?ex=1099022400&en=7029c a0373f5d4d0&ei=5070&oref=login*].

[105] DHS press release, "Ridge Creates New Division to Combat Cyber Threats," June 6, 2003, [*http://www.dhs.gov/dhspublic/display?content =916*].

[106] Statement by Amit Yoran, Director National Cyber Security Division Department of Homeland Security before the U.S. Senate Committee on the Judiciary Subcommittee on Terrorism, Technology, and Homeland Security, February 24, 2004, [*http://www.us-cert.gov/ policy/testimony_yoran_feb2404.html#nature*].

[107] Patience Wait, "Industry asks Congress for help on DHS cybersecurity role", *Washington Technology*, October 15, 2004, [*http://www. washingtontechnology.com/news/1_1/homeland/24745-1.html*].

[108] Agencies operating national security systems are required to purchase software products from a list of lab-tested and evaluated products in a program run by the National Information Assurance Partnership (NIAP), a joint partnership between the National Security Agency and the National Institute of Standards and Technology. The NIAP is the U.S. government program that works with organizations in a dozen other countries around the world which have endorsed the international security-evaluation regimen known as the "Common Criteria." The program requires vendors to submit software for review in an accredited lab, a process that often takes a year and costs several thousand dollars. The review previously was limited to military national security software and equipment, however, the Administration has stated that the government will undertake a review of the program to "possibly extend" this software certification requirement to civilian agencies. Ellen Messmer,, White House issue "National Strategy to Secure Cyberspace," *Network World Fusion*, February 14, 2003 [*http://www.nwfusion.com/news/2003/0214ntl strategy.html*].

[109] Business executives may be cautious about spending for large new technology projects, such as placing new emphasis on computer security. Results from a February 2003 survey of business executives indicated that 45 percent of respondents believed that many large Information Technology (IT) projects are often too expensive to justify. Managers in the survey pointed to the estimated $125.9 billion dollars spent on IT projects between 1977 and 2000 in preparation for the year 2000 (Y2K) changeover, now viewed by some as a nonevent. Sources reported that some board-level executives stated that the Y2K problem was overblown and over funded then, and as a result, they are now much more cautious about future spending for any new, massive IT initiatives. Gary H. Anthes and Thomas Hoffman, "Tarnished Image," *Computerworld*, May 12, 2003, vol. 37, no. 19, p. 37.

[110] Howard Schmidt points out that major technology firms now promote anti-virus software and encourage better cybersecurity practices. He stresses that

market forces are causing private industry to improve security of products. Martin Kady, "Cybersecurity a Weak Link in Homeland's Armor," *CQ Weekly*, Feb. 14, 2005. Meanwhile, Richard Clarke, who initially opposed regulation during his tenure in the Clinton and Bush administrations, now states that the IT industry only reponds to improve security of its products when regulation is threatened. William Jackson, "To Regulate or Not to Regulate? That Is the Question," *Government Computer News*, Feb. 26, 2005.

[111] Building in more security adds to the cost of a software product. Now that software features are similar across brands, software vendors have indicated that their customers, including federal government agencies, often make purchases based largely on product price. *Conference on Software Product Security Features*, Information Assurance Technical Information Framework Forum, Laurel, Maryland, NSA, 2001.

[112] A 2004 survey of 329 PC users revealed that most computer users think they are safe but lack basic protections against viruses, spyware, hackers, and other online threats. In addition, large majorities of home computer users have been infected with viruses and spyware and remain highly vulnerable to future infections. AOL and the National Cyber Security Alliance, "Largest In-home Study of Home Computer Users Shows Major Online Threats, Perception Gap," Oct. 2004, [*http://www.staysafeonline.info/news/NCSA-AOLIn-HomeStudyRelease.pdf*].

[113] A spokesperson for the Computer Emergency Response Team at Carnegie Mellon has reportedly stated that most people may not yet realize that anti-virus software and a firewall are no longer enough to protect computers anymore. Charles Duhigg, "Fight Against Viruses May Move to Servers," *Washington Post*, Aug. 28, 2003, p. E01.

[114] Government Accountability Office, *Homeland Security: Efforts To Improve Information Sharing Need to Be Strengthened*, GAO-03-760, August 2003.

[115] CRS Report RL30153, *Critical Infrastructures: Background, Policy and Implementation*, by John Moteff,

[116] Trace back to identify a cyberattacker at the granular level remains problematic. Dorothy Denning, *Information Warfare and Security*, (Addison-Wesley, 1999), p. 217.

[117] In Argentina, a group calling themselves the X-Team, hacked into the website of that country's Supreme Court in April 2002. The trial judge stated that the law in his country covers crime against people, things, and animals but not websites. The group on trial was declared not guilty of breaking into the website. Paul Hillbeck, "Argentine Judge Rules in Favor

of Computer Hackers, Feb. 5, 2002, [*http://www.sili convalley.com/mld/siliconvalley/news/editorial/3070194.htm*].

[118] Abraham D. Sofaer, et.al., The Hoover Institution, The Consortium for Research on Information Security and Policy (CRISP), and The Center for International Security and Cooperation (CISAC) Stanford University, "A Proposal for an International Convention on Cyber Crime and Terrorism," August   2000,   [http://www.iwar.org.uk /law/resources/cybercrime/stanford/cisac-draft.htm].

[119] In 2000, news sources reported that the Defense Agency of Japan halted the introduction of a new computer system after discovering that some of the software had been developed by members of the Aum Shinrikyo cult, which was responsible for the fatal 1995 Tokyo subway gas attack. The Defense Agency was one of 90 government agencies and industry firms that had ordered software produced by the cult. Richard Power, *Current & Future Danger: A CSI Primer on Computer Crime and Information Warfare*, Computer Security Institute, 2000.

[120] Dan Verton, "Offshore Coding Work Raises Security Concerns," *Computerworld*, May 5, 2003, vol. 37, no. 18, p. 1.

[121] Under FISMA, the Director of OMB: oversees the implementation of information security policies for civilian federal agencies, requires agencies to identify and provide information security protection appropriate for the level of risk and magnitude of harm resulting from possible destruction of information or systems, and coordinates the development of security standards and guidelines developed between NIST, NSA, and other agencies to assure they are complementary with standards and guidelines developed for national security systems. See 44 U.S.C., Section 3543 (a).

[122] Using these five basic steps, often supplemented with automated intrusion tools, attackers have successfully taken over computer systems and remained undetected for long periods of time. Ed Skoudis, *Counter Hack*, (New Jersey: Prentice Hall, 2002).

[123] These include Ed Skoudis, *Counter Hack: A Step-By-Step Guide to Computer Attacks and Effective Defenses*, (New Jersey: Prentice Hall, 2002); Winn Schwartau, *Information Warfare Cyberterrorism: Protecting Your Personal Security in the Electronic Age*, (Publishers Group West, 1996); and Jeff Crume, *Inside Internet Security: What Hackers Don't Want You To Know*, (Pearson Education Limited, 2000).

[124] For more about Spyware, see Spywareinfo at [*http://www.spywareinfo. com/*].

[125] An attacker may use an automatic "War Dialing" tool that dials thousands of telephone numbers, looking for modems connected to a computer. If a computer modem answers when the War Dialer calls, the attacker may have located a way to enter an organization's network and bypass firewall security. A newer way of scanning for vulnerabilities is called "War Driving", where hackers drive randomly through a neighborhood trying to detect signals from business or home wireless networks. Once a network is detected, the hacker may park nearby and attempt to log on to gain free, unauthorized access. Kevin Poulsen, "War Driving by the Bay," Securityfocus.com, April 12, 2001, [*http://www.securityfocus.com/news/192*].

[126] New "antiforensics tools" are now available on the Internet that allow hackers to more effectively hide their actions, and thus defeat more investigators who search for technical evidence of computer intrusions. Anne Saita, "Antiforensics: The Looming Arms Race," *Information Security*, May 2003, vol. 6, no. 5, p.13.

[127] In September 2003, DHS warned U.S. industry and the federal government to expect potentially significant attacks to emerge against Internet operations, similar to the recent Blaster worm exploit, because of newly discovered critical flaws in Windows software that were announced by Microsoft Corporation. Jaikumar Vijayan, "Attacks on New Windows Flaws Expected Soon," *Computerworld*, Sept. 15, 2003, vol. 37, no. 37, p. 1.

[128] A single reported computer security incident may involve one site or hundreds (or even thousands) of sites. Also, some incidents may involve ongoing activity for long periods of time. CERT estimates that as much as 80 percent of actual security incidents goes unreported, in most cases because the organization was unable to recognize that its systems had been penetrated or there were no indications of penetration or attack; or the organization was reluctant to publicly admit to being a victim of a computer security breach. CERT, 2003, "CERT/CC Statistics 1988-2002," April 15, 2003, [*http://www.cert. org/stats/cert_stats.html#incidents.*] "CERT/CC Statistics, 2003," [*http://www.cert.org/ stats/cert_stats.html*].

[129] MARC Commuter and CSX freight rail service experienced cancellations and delays on August 21, 2003, because of a virus that disabled the computer systems at the CSX railway Jacksonville, Florida headquarters. The "Blaster" computer worm attacked more than 500,000 computers worldwide within one week. The "Blaster" attack was quickly followed the next week by another worm that spread worldwide, called "Welchia," which

installed itself on computers by taking advantage of the same vulnerability used by Blaster. Brian Krebs, "'Good' Worm Fixes Infected Computers," Washingtonpost.com, Aug. 18, 2003. The "Welchia" worm also disrupted the highly secure Navy Marine Corps Intranet (NMCI) during the week of August 11, by flooding it with unwanted traffic. This was the first time that military network was disrupted by an outside cyberattack. Diane Frank, "Attack of the Worms: Feds Get Wake-Up Call," *Federal Computer Week*, Aug. 25, 2003, vol. 17, no. 29, p. 8.

[130] The FBI is investigating what private security experts believe to be the first Internet attack aimed primarily at a single economic sector. The malicious code, discovered in June 2003, contains a list of roughly 1,200 Web addresses for many of the world's largest financial institutions, including J.P. Morgan Chase & Co., American Express Co., Wachovia Corp., Bank of America Corp. and Citibank N.A. "Bugbear" is a polymorphic worm/virus that has keystroke-logging and mass-mailing capabilities, and attempts to terminate various antivirus and firewall programs. Though most major banks do not put sensitive information on the Internet, the worm will attempt to use information captured from a desktop PC to break into restricted computers that do contain financial data. For example, experts found that the Bugbear software is programmed to determine whether a victim used an e-mail address that belonged to any of the 1,300 financial institutions listed in its blueprints. If a match is made, it tries to steal passwords and other information that would make it easier for hackers to break into a bank's networks. The software then transmits stolen passwords to 10 e-mail addresses, which also are included in the blueprints. But experts said that on the Internet anyone can easily open a free e-mail account using a false name, and so knowing those addresses might not lead detectives to the culprit. A.P., "Feds Warn Banks About Internet Attack," CNN.Com,   June   10,   2003, [*http://www.cnn.com/2003/TECH/internet/06/10/virus.banks.ap/index.html*].

[131] The Naval Postgraduate School is developing a new network security tool called "Therminator" that is designed to detect possible computer attacks by carefully monitoring network traffic. Jason Ma, "NPS Touts Therminator As Early-Warning Tool for Computer Attacks," *Inside the Navy*, Navy-16-40-12, Oct. 6, 2003.

[132] The "Slammer" worm attacked Microsoft's database software and spread through the Internet over one weekend in January 2003. According to a preliminary study coordinated by the Cooperative Association for Internet Data Analysis (CAIDA), on January 25, 2003, the SQL Slammer worm

(also known as "Sapphire") infected more than 90 percent of vulnerable computers worldwide within 10 minutes of its release on the Internet, making it the fastest computer worm in history. As the study reports, exploiting a known vulnerability for which a patch has been available since July 2002, Slammer doubled in size every 8.5 seconds and achieved its full scanning rate (55 million scans per second) after about 3 minutes. It caused considerable harm through network outages and such unforeseen consequences as canceled airline flights and automated teller machine (ATM) failures. Further, the study emphasizes that the effects would likely have been more severe had Slammer carried a malicious payload, attacked a more widespread vulnerability, or targeted a more popular service. The malicious code disrupted more than 13,000 Bank of America automated teller machines, causing some machines to stop issuing money, and took most of South Korea Internet users offline. As many as five of the 13 Internet root name servers were also slowed or disabled, according to Anti-virus firm F-Secure. Robert F. Dacey, "INFORMATION SECURITY: Progress Made, But Challenges Remain to Protect Federal Systems and the Nation's Critical Infrastructures," 2003; Matt Loney, "Slammer attacks may become way of life for Net ," *Cnet.News.com,* Feb. 6, 2003, [*http://news.com.com/Damage+control/2009-1001_3-983540.html*]; Robert Lemos, "Worm exposes apathy, Microsoft flaws," Cnet.News.com, Jan. 26, 2003 [*http://news.com.com/2102-1001-9821 35.html*].

[133] "Report to Congress Regarding the Terrorism Information Awareness Program," *Executive Summary*, May 20, 2003, p.3.

[134] Jerry Seper, "'Sleeper Cells' of Al Qaeda Active in U.S. Despite War," *Washington Times*, Feb. 11, 2004, [*http://www.washington times.com/national/20040210-105654-8823r.htm*].

[135] U.S. Citizen Services, "Travel Warnings and Warden Messages," June 16, 2004, [*http://riyadh.usembassy.gov/saudi-arabia/w1504.html*].

INDEX

D

E

J

K

L

M

N

O

P